I0421359

Adventurous Ants Coloring and Activity Book

Coloring Pages, Mazes, Word Searches, and More!

A "Critter Activity Book"
by Julia L. Wright
from HieroGraphics Books.

Published by HieroGraphics Books as part of the "Critters Activity Book" collection created by Julia L. Wright.

No part of this publication may be reproduced, stored in a retrieval system, or transmitted in any means, electronic, photocopying, recording, or otherwise without the prior permission of the publisher by emailing info@hierographicsbooksllc.com.

It is acceptable to copy a maze page for your personal use, but it may not be shared with others without permission from the publisher.

If after a young person colors a page and he or she wants to remove a page for framing, please ask an adult to carefully cut it out with a very sharp knife and a ruler.

For information regarding permissions, write to:
info@hierographicsbooksllc.com

www.hierographicsbooksllc.com
Manitou Springs, CO

Cover Design by Julia L. Wright ©2020

Copyright ©Hierographics Books LLC
All Rights Reserved

Printed in the United States of America

First Printing, February, 2021

ISBN: 978-0-9965816-9-1

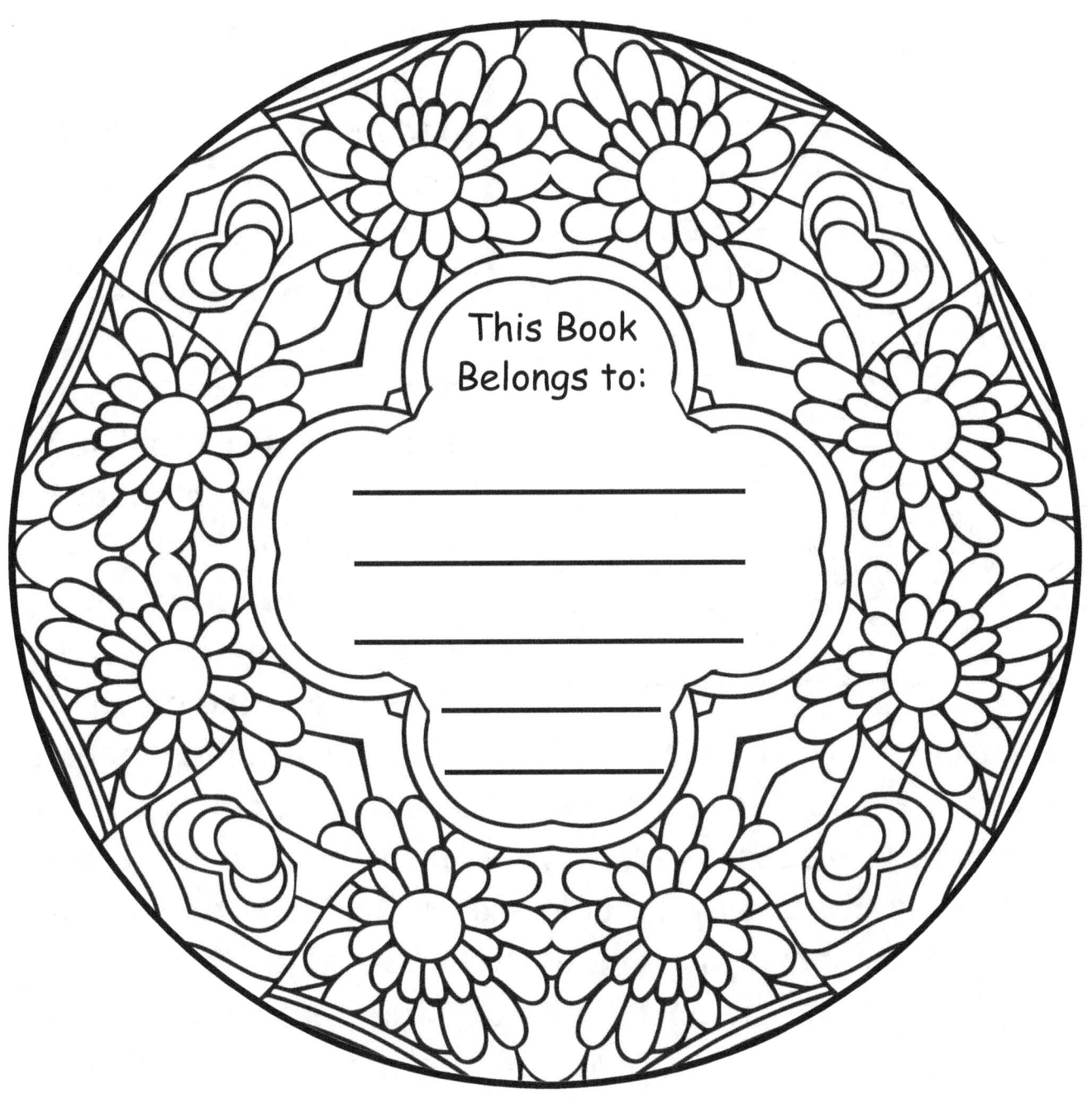

This Book
Belongs to:

_____

_____

_____

_____

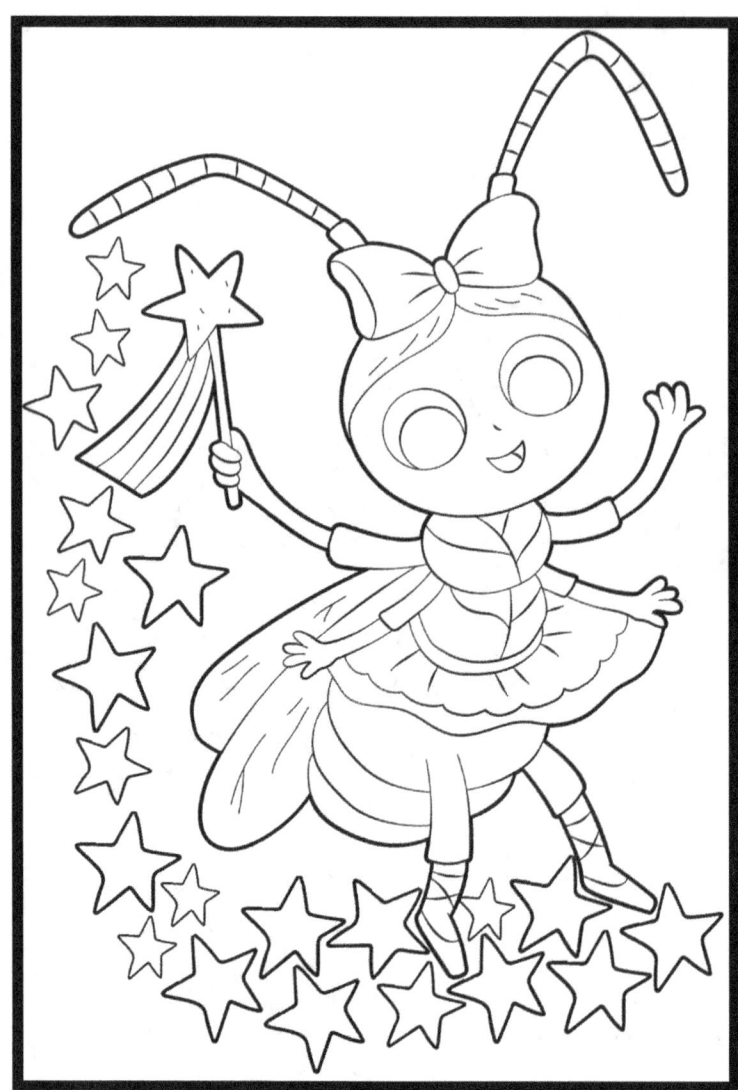

Annie Ant would like to tell you a little about what you will find inside this coloring and activity book. She knows you must appreciate ants because you brought this book home to have some fun by coloring them.

Each Adventurous Ant has been given a name and there is a very short story about what they are doing on the page they appear upon.

Some Adventurous Ants are bolder in what they are doing on their adventures outside the anthill. Others have tamer ideas of what it means to have an adventure away from their home.

There are Mazes and two types of Word Puzzles to solve as activities to do beyond coloring these Adventurous Ants.

The Mazes have just one path for each ant to follow to be able to leave the anthill and go start their adventures. They need your help to discover that path. If you find the Mazes in this activity book challenging, you might want to copy them to work on outside of the book.

When doing the Word Search Puzzles, you will be circling the words listed above the puzzle found among a random series of letters. Some will be straight across, others will be found on an angle or spelled in a backwards manner.

One Word Search Puzzle is based on the names of the ants in this coloring book. The second Word Search Puzzle has words that relate to what one of the Adventurous Ants is doing away from their anthill.

The first Crossword Puzzle will ask you to respond with the name of an Adventurous Ant that is doing a specific activity on one of the pages. The clues for the second one relate to a scene or an activity that an Adventurous Ant is engaged in somewhere in this book.

When you draw a line by following the numbered dots you will reveal which Adventurous Ant will be seen on that page. They have a border to color around them.

There are some pages with rectangular patterns to color.

When coloring, remember these are your images to create and make them look however you like to color. Some have areas of very tiny lines, but you don't have to color in each small section. You may chose that area to be just one color, or color every other one of the tiny sections. This is meant to be a fun activity book, and maybe just a little challenging.

To learn more about these fascinating insects read the article with interesting facts about Ants.

At the end of this book are pages where a budding author can write stories about what their favorite Adventurous Ants are doing. Aspiring artists have a space they can use to sketch an image for that story.

So it's time to start coloring Adventurous Ants in the scenes they are adventuring in or a patterned design, or engage in some of the activities you will find inside.

HAVE FUN!

What You Will Find On The Pages In This Adventurous Ants Coloring And Activity Book:

On Pages 7 to 25 you can color Adventurous Ants engaged in many different adventures.

On Pages 27 to 37 are Mazes to solve to guide a an Adventurous Ant out of their anthill.

On Pages 39 to 53 you will be coloring four Adventurous Ants in two different scenes on their adventures.

Page 55 has a Word Search Puzzle using the names of the Adventurous Ants.

Page 57 has a Word Search of Glossary Words relating to an Adventurous Ant's adventure.

On Pages 59 to 71 you will draw lines between the numbered dots to reveal the Adventurous Ant that is standing inside a patterned border you can color.

Page 72 has clues for a Crossword Puzzle for you to name the Adventurous Ant that is engaged in one of the adventures described there.

Page 74 has clues for a Crossword Puzzle relating to what an Adventurous Ant is doing.

On Pages 77 to 89 there are rectangular designs to color.

Pages 93 to 103 have the Solutions for the Adventurous Ants Mazes.

Page 107 has the Solution for the Adventurous Ants Names Word Search on page 55.

Page 109 has the Solution for the Adventurous Ants Glossary Word Search on page 57.

Page 109 has the Answers for the Adventurous Ants Names Crossword Puzzle on page 73.

Page 111 has the Answers for the Adventurous Ants Glossary Crossword Puzzle on page 75.

Pages 112 and 113 there are some book suggestions that kids who love Nature might enjoy.

On Pages 114-116 there is an article with some interesting facts about Ants.

Pages 117, 119, 121, 123 and 125 offers places for budding writers to "Write a Story" about their favorite Adventurous Ant they found in this book.

Pages 118, 120, 122 and 124 have spaces for aspiring artists to draw images relating to the story they wrote or create a new illustration of a Adventurous Ant in a different environment.

Victor is a very adventurous ant. He brought his machetes to help him explore the jungle filled with tall grass on a search to find interesting bugs or creatures in the wild.

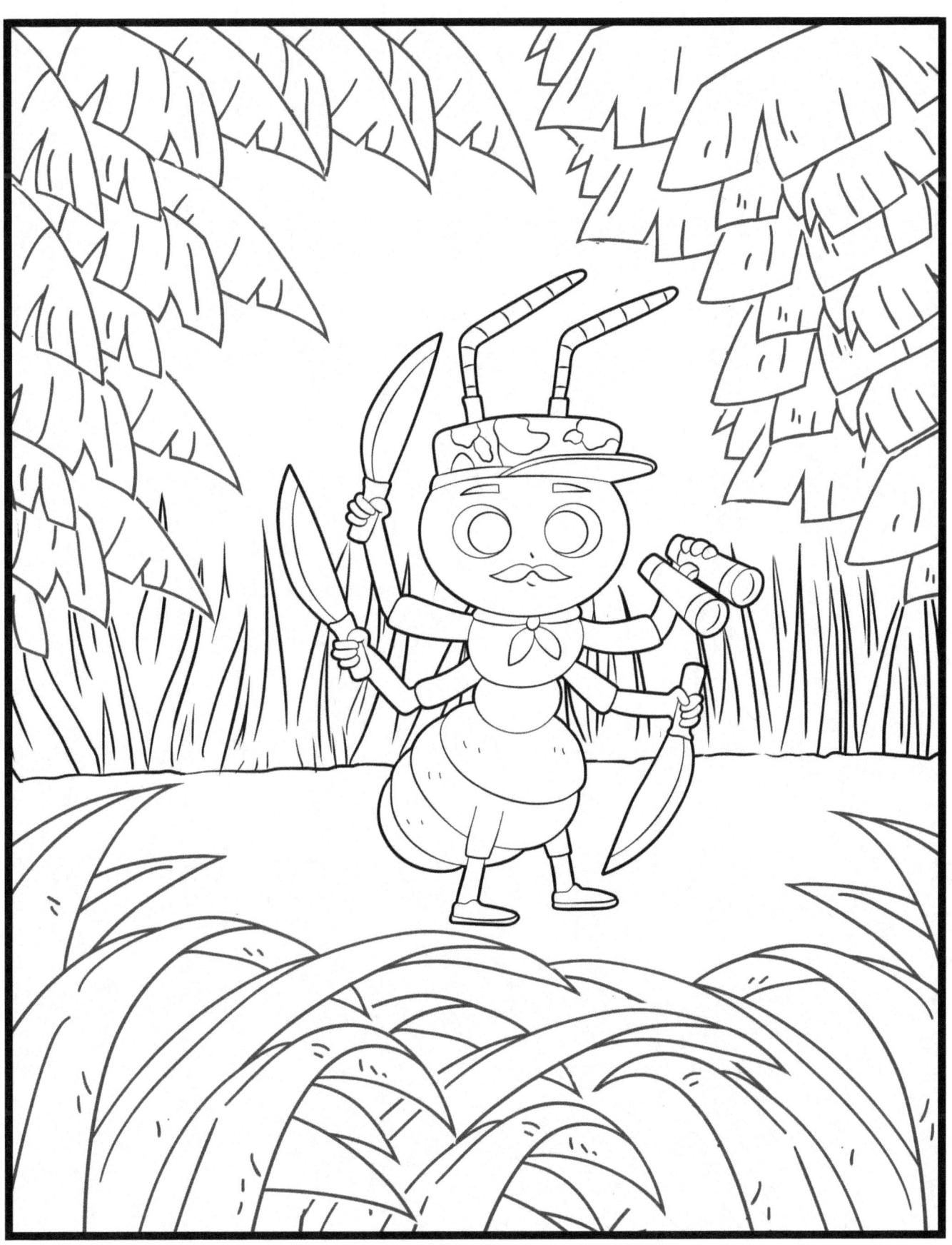

Wanda left the anthill to catch a butterfly with her net, but thinks they are more beautiful flying freely in the sky. So, she decided just to pick a flower to bring back home.

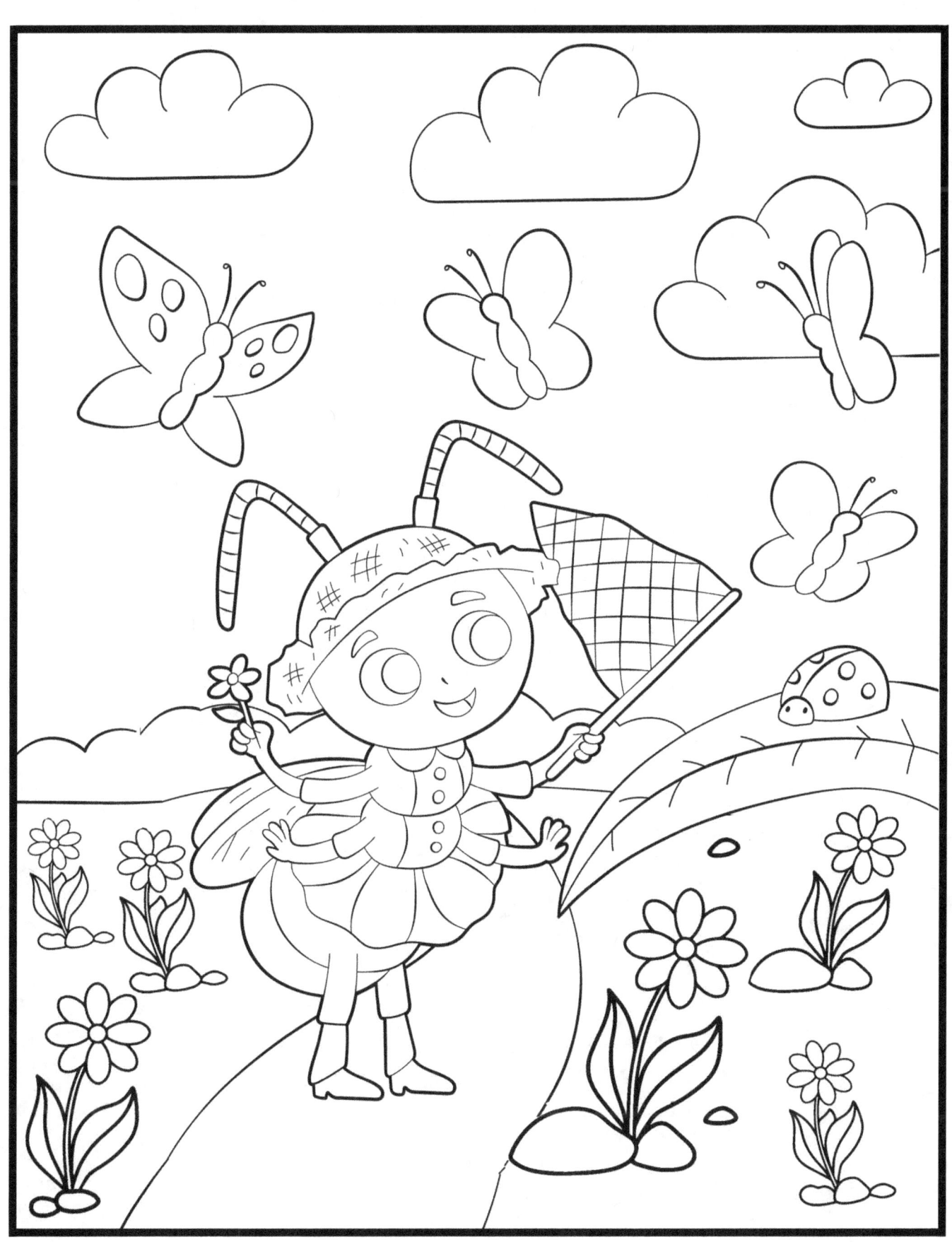

As the sun sets in the west, **Peter** rests on his shovel admiring the flowers he planted in his garden that day.

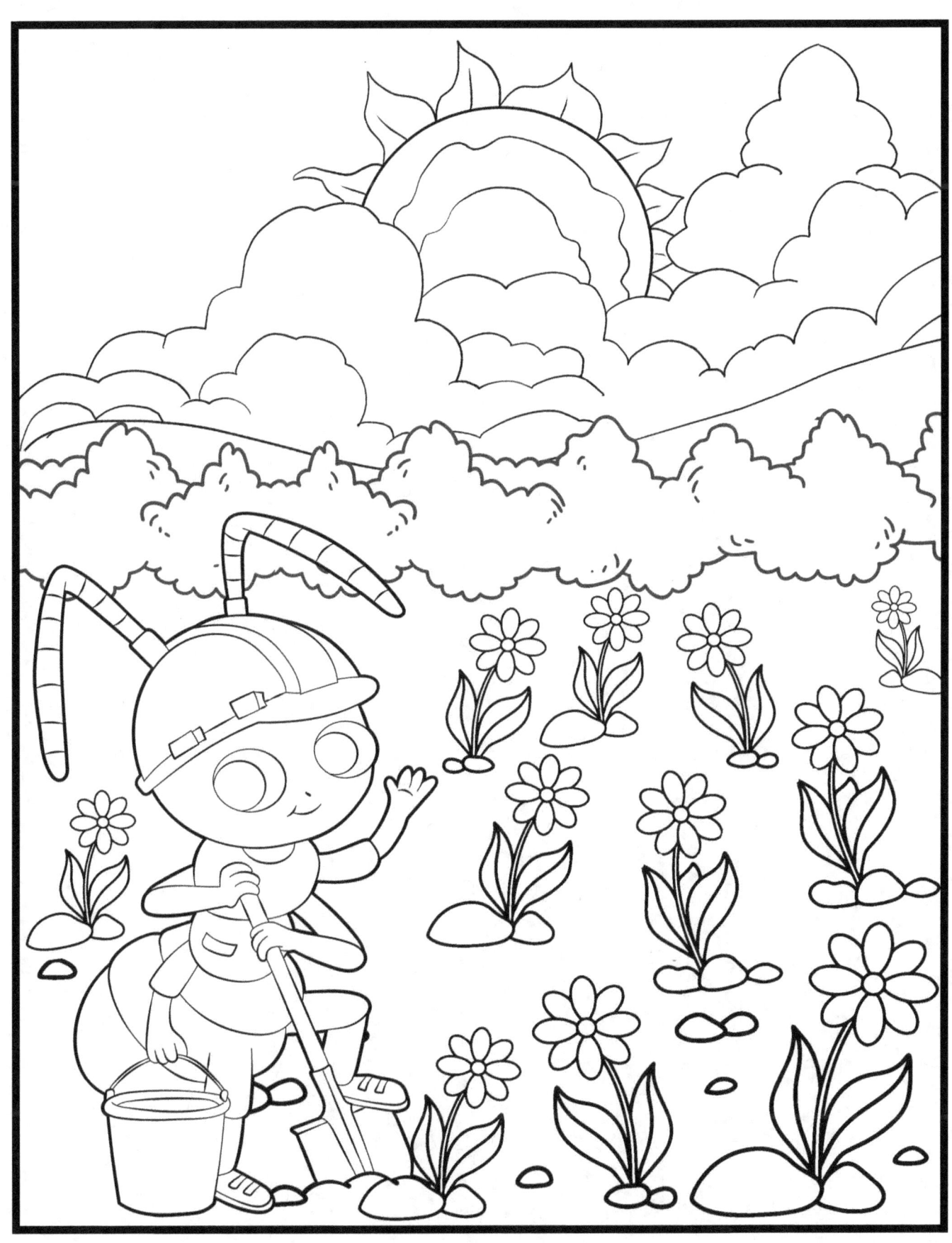

Liam is practicing walking on a tightrope. He wants to amaze his adventurous friends at a party when he performs this balancing act on a thin rope higher up in the air.

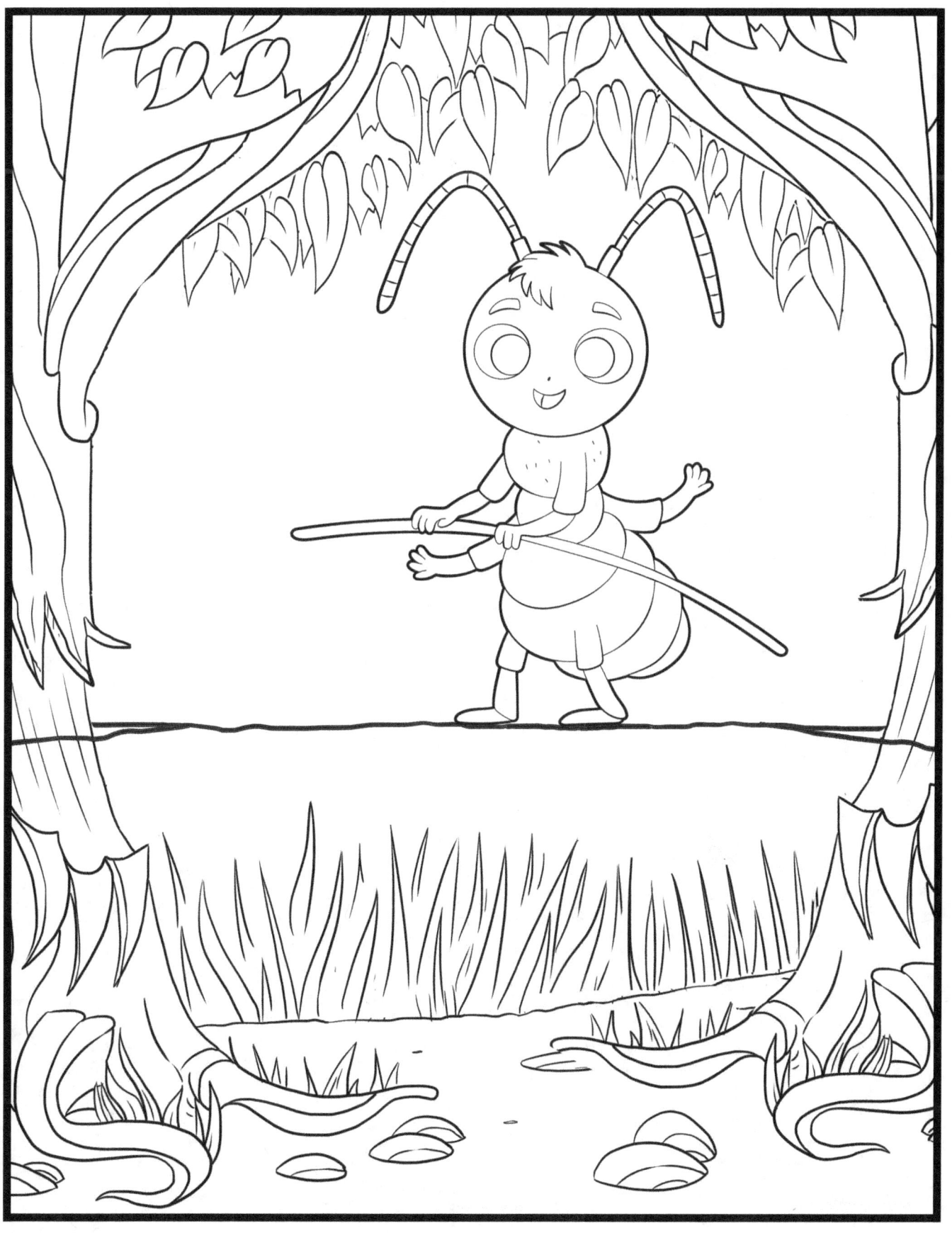

Zara found a lovely place to do a ceremonial dance around a fire. It was a safe distance from the forest trees near a river in a beautiful mountain valley.

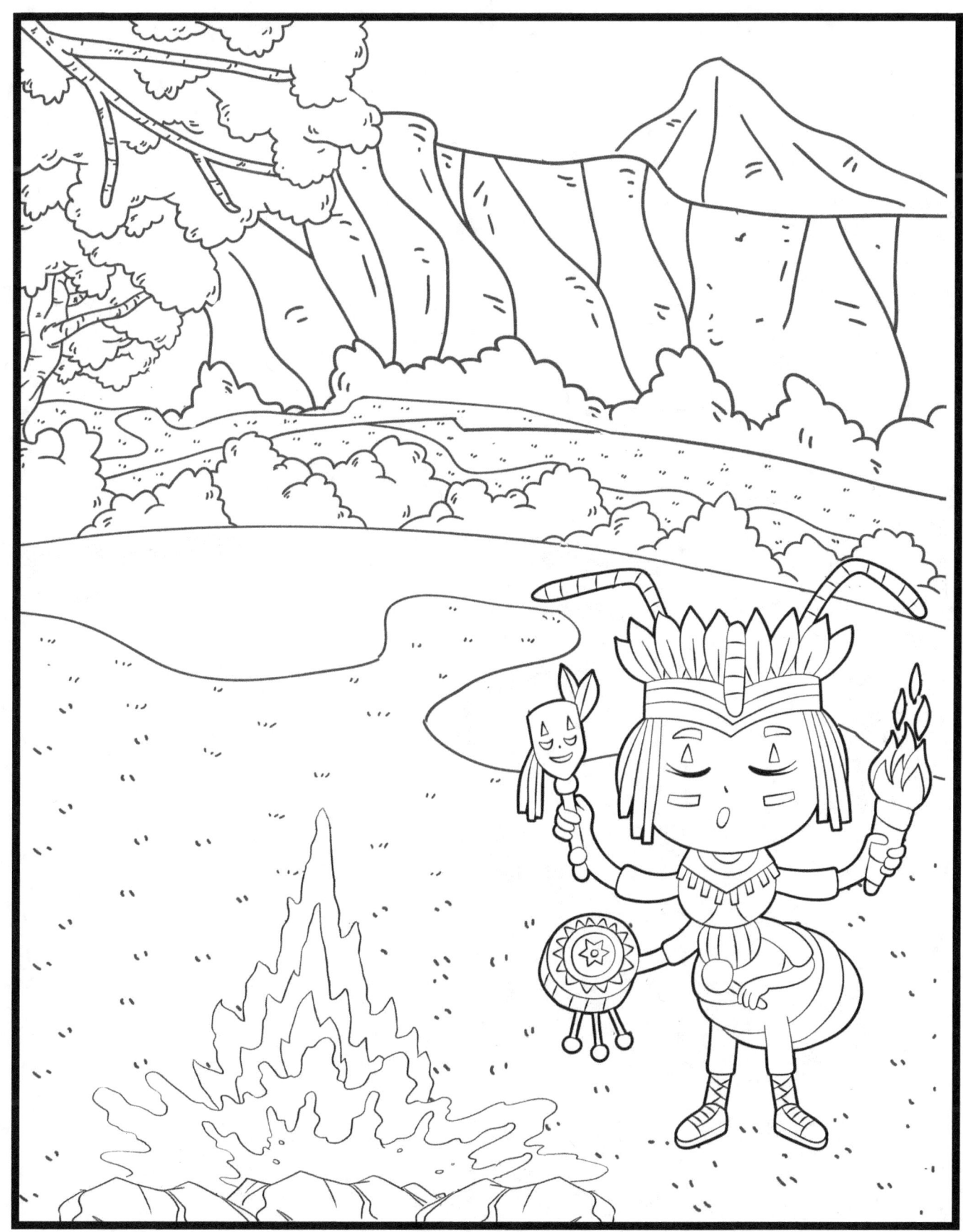

Olivia and Ciara are having a party in a field of flowers. They met here today to enjoy some cake and celebrate their birthdays together on this lovely summer day.

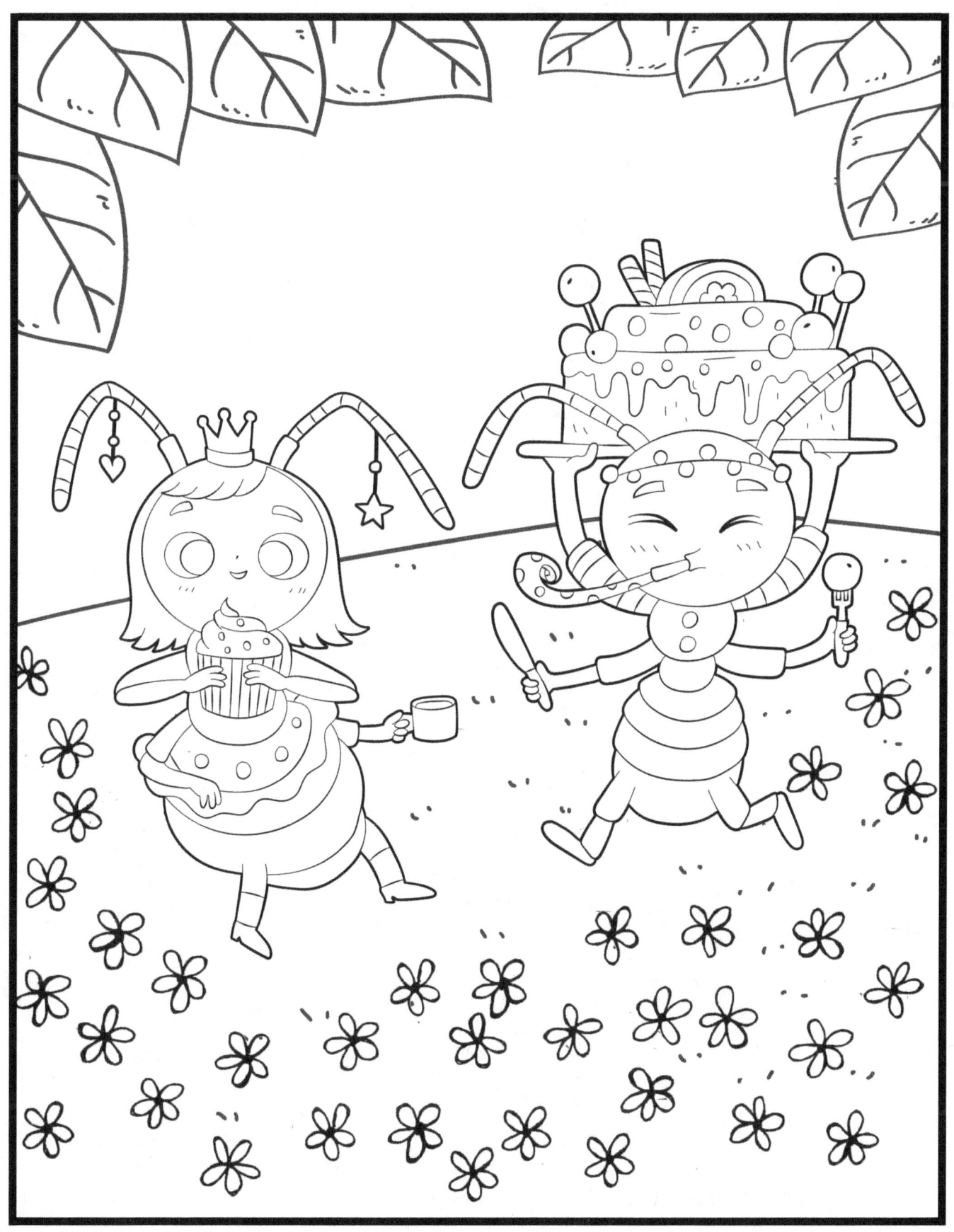

Mike had a fun adventure climbing on hay bales near a barn. He discovered he could reach plenty of apples from a nearby tree to fill a basket he will use to carry them to his home.

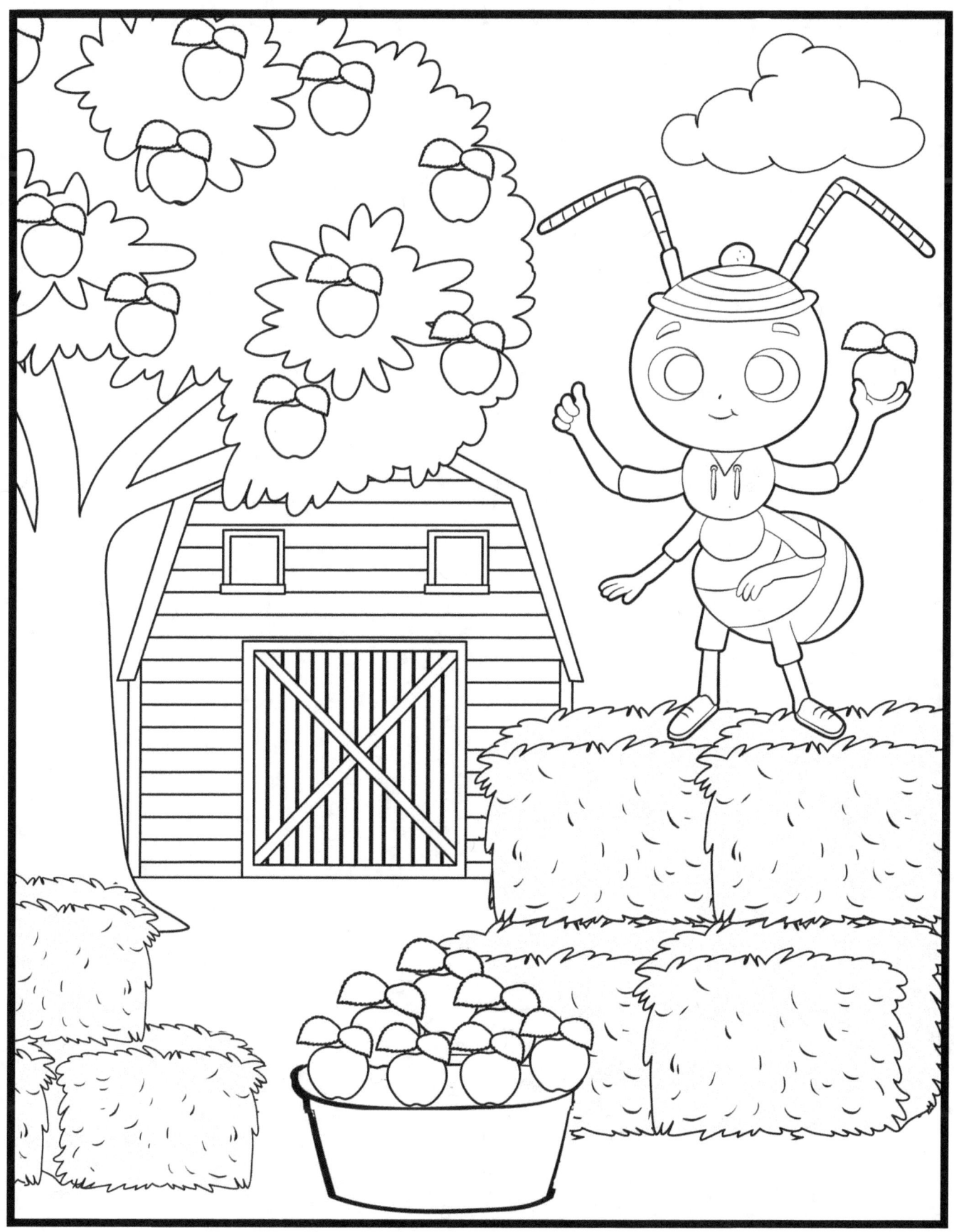

Izabel's idea of adventure involves finding a shady place next to a stream in the forest to enjoy slices of watermelon and a cold drink.

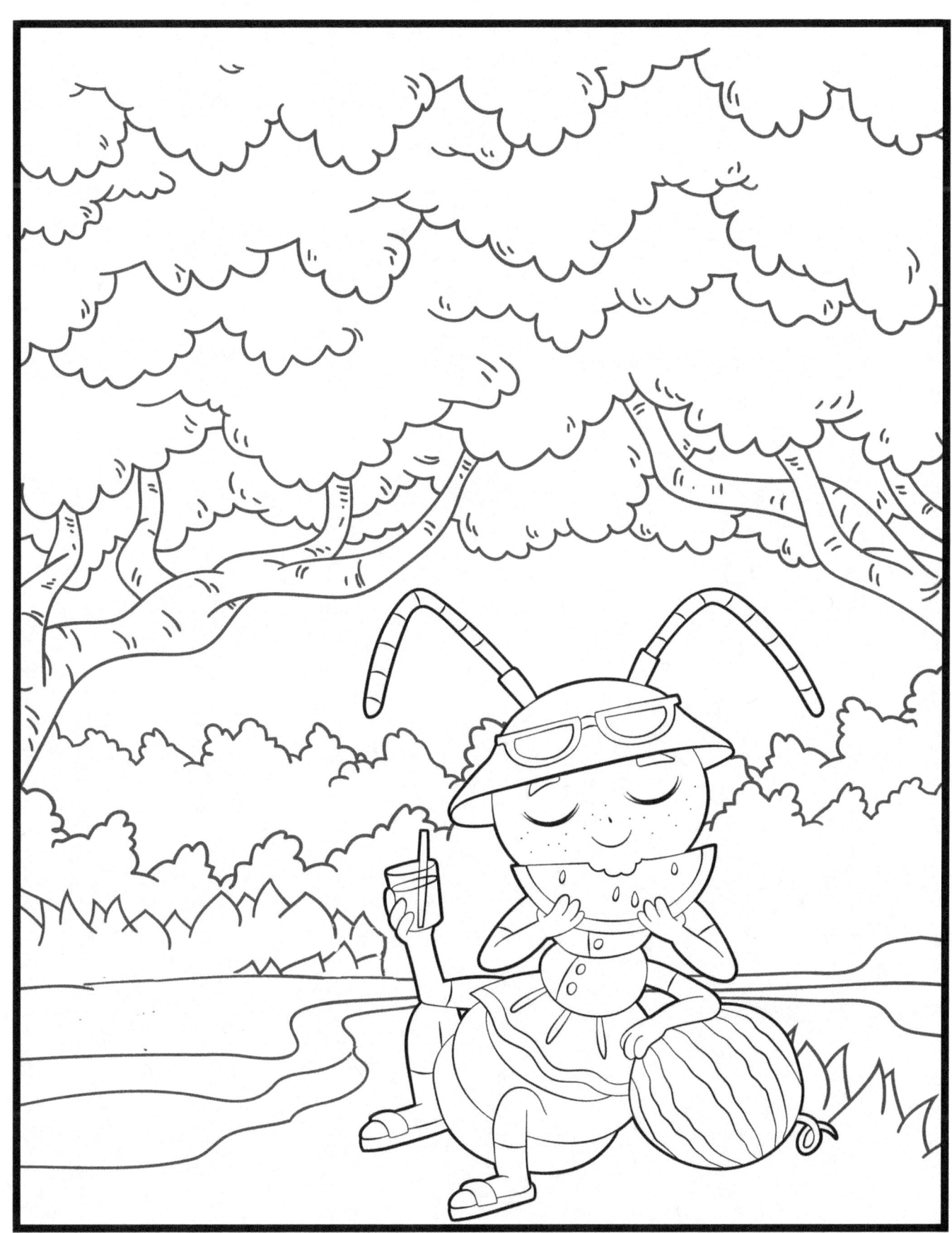

Edgar followed a map of the forest to find a beehive.
He was happy to spend time watching bees and butterflies
flying above him while sitting on a lovely big flower.

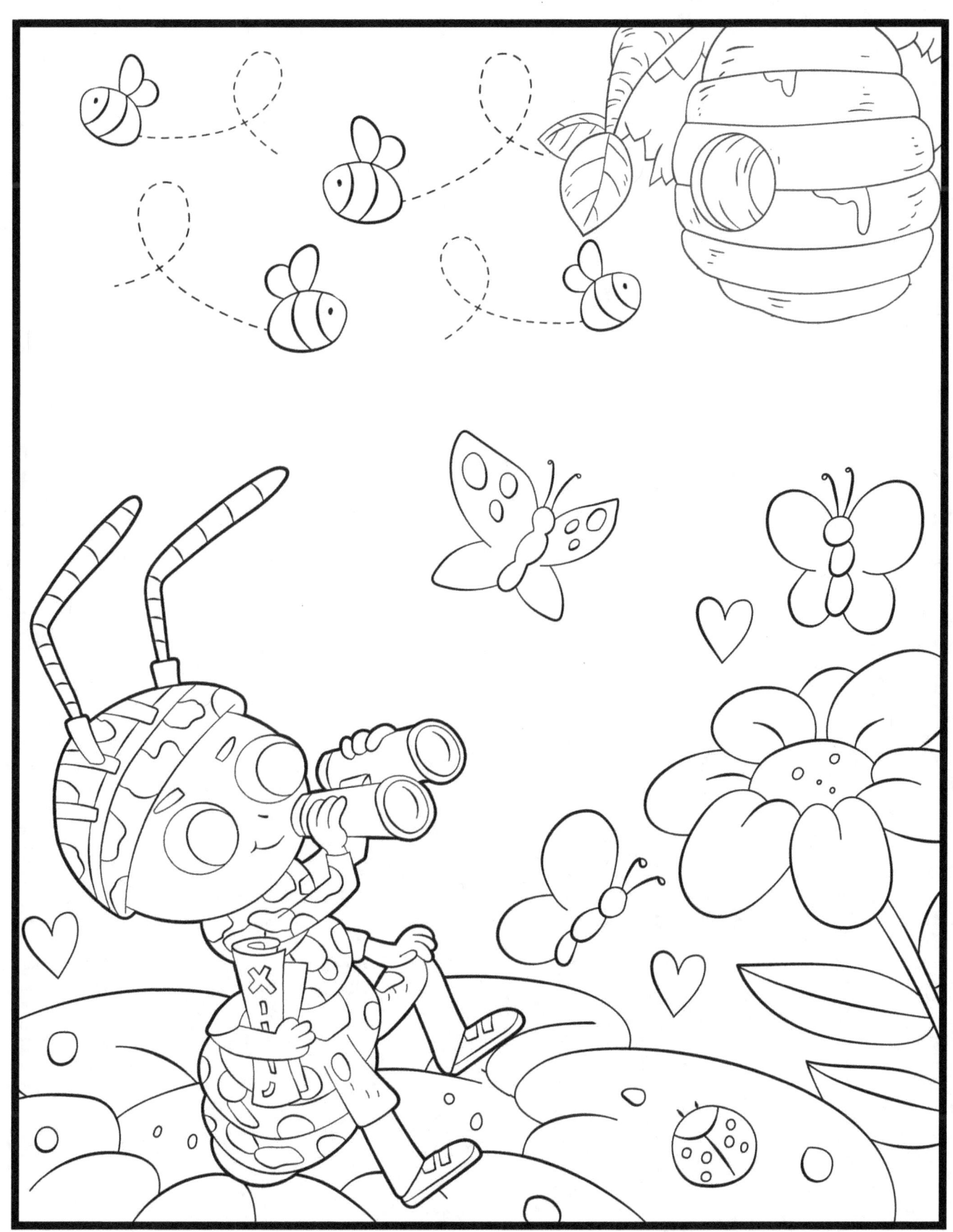

Annie got dressed as a fairy princess to explore a dream she had last night. It led her to take a walk up this path leading to a castle nestled on a cloud in the star-filled night sky.

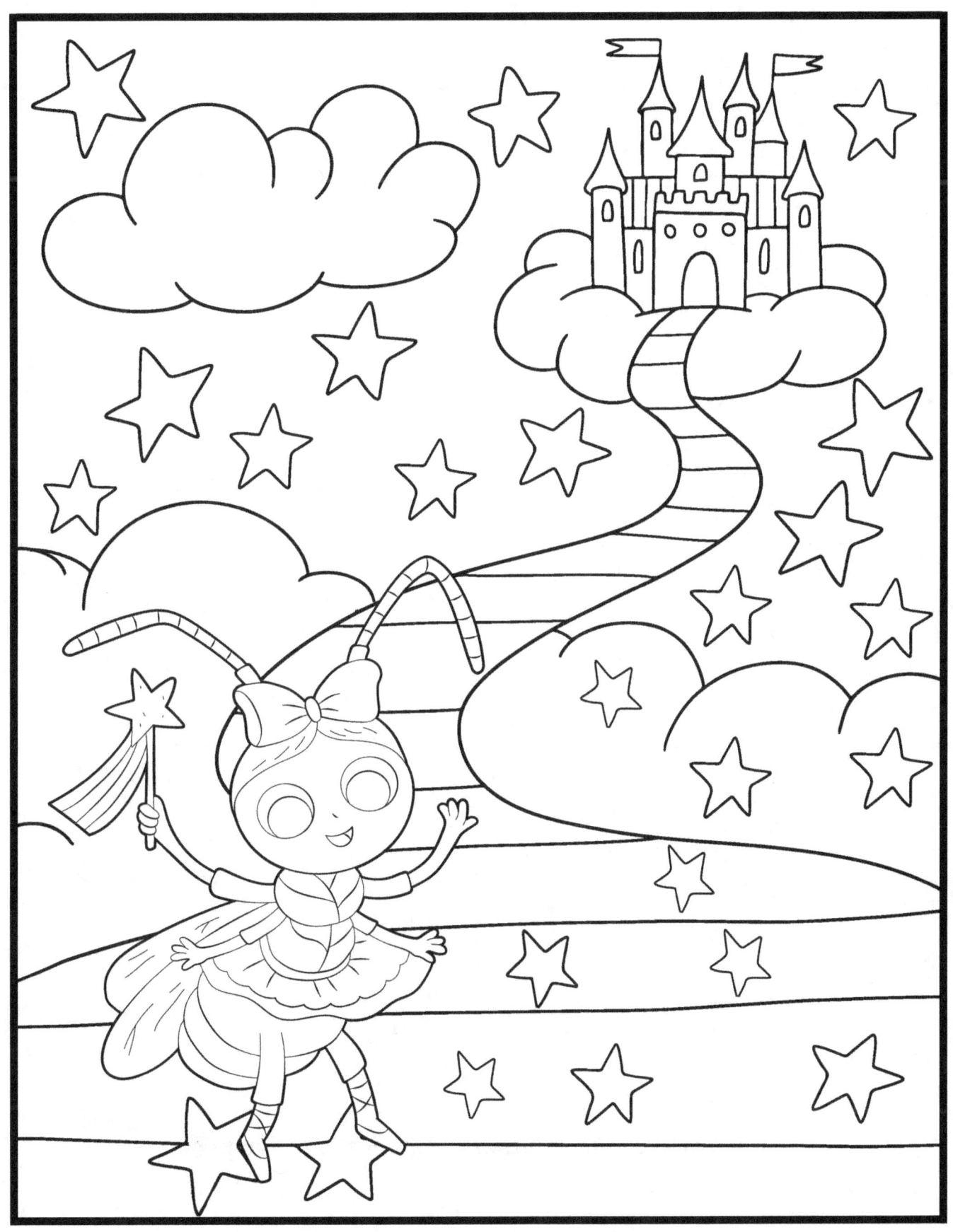

You can find the Solution to Izabel's maze on page 93.

Izabel is dressed to go swimming on this sunny day, but she needs your help to find the path out of the anthill.

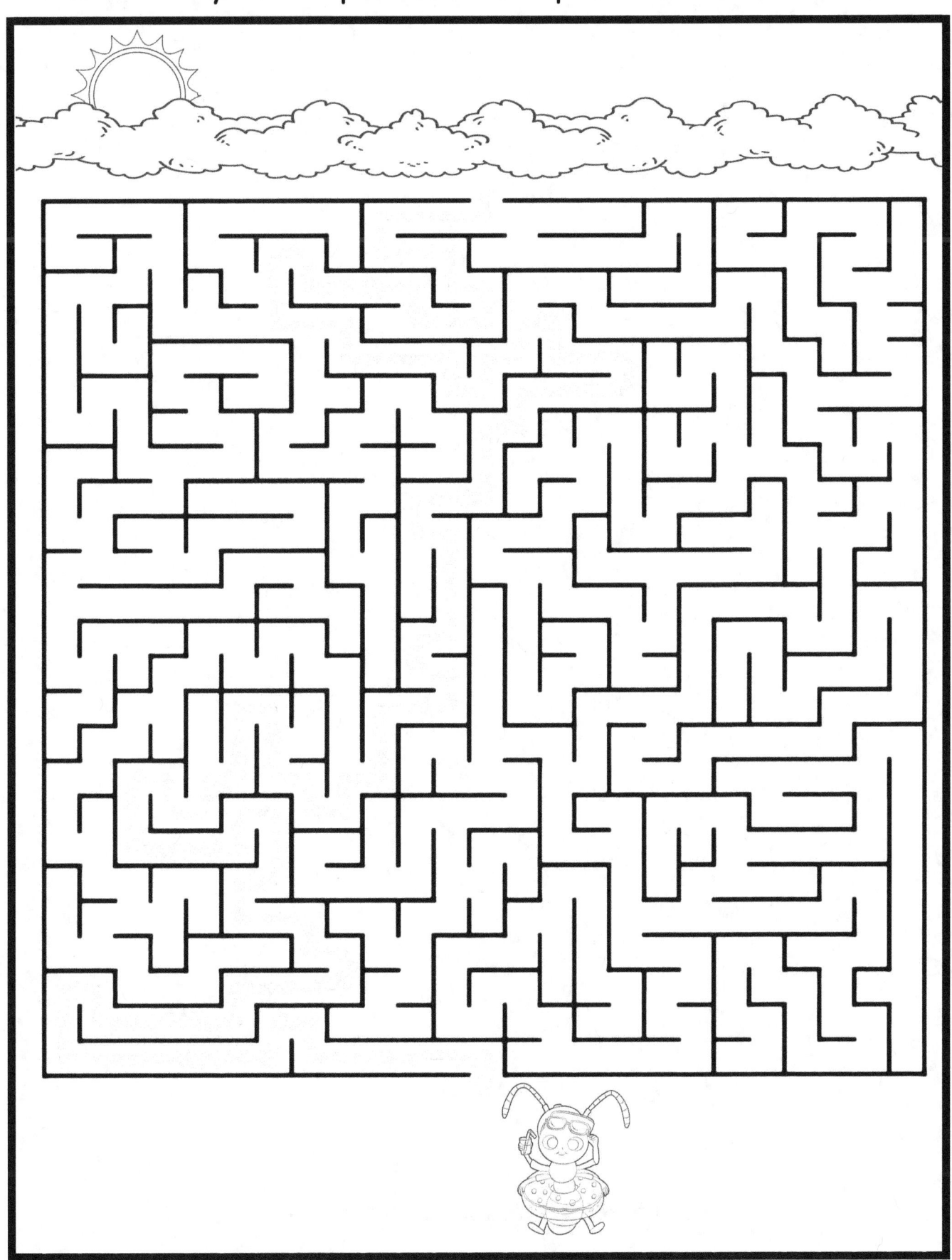

You can find the Solution to this maze on page 95.

Victor is ready to go exploring in the jungle, but can't find the correct path out of the anthill. Can you help him?

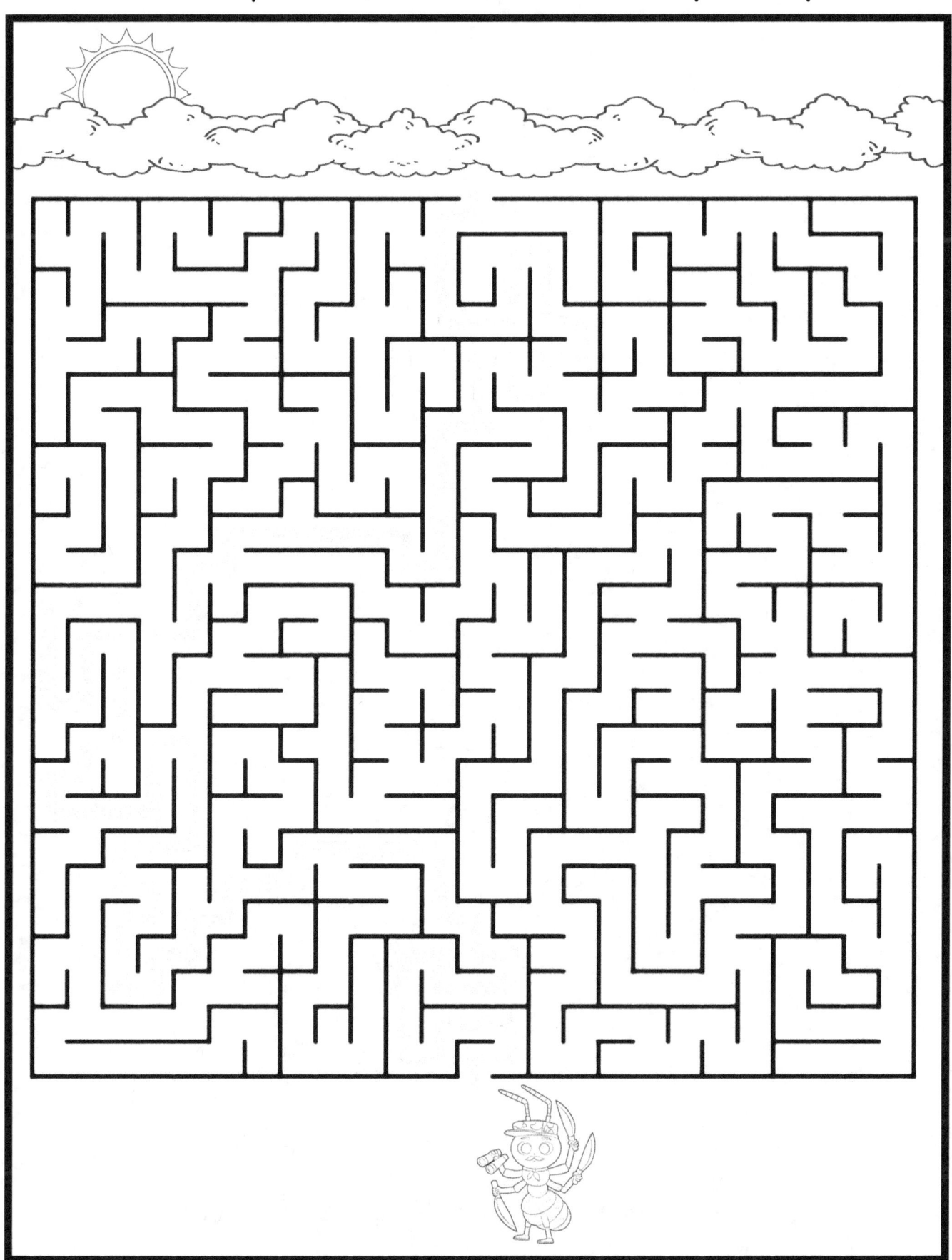

You can find the Solution to this maze on page 97.

Mike wants to go harvest more apples but is a little lost.
Will you help him find the path to take to leave the anthill?

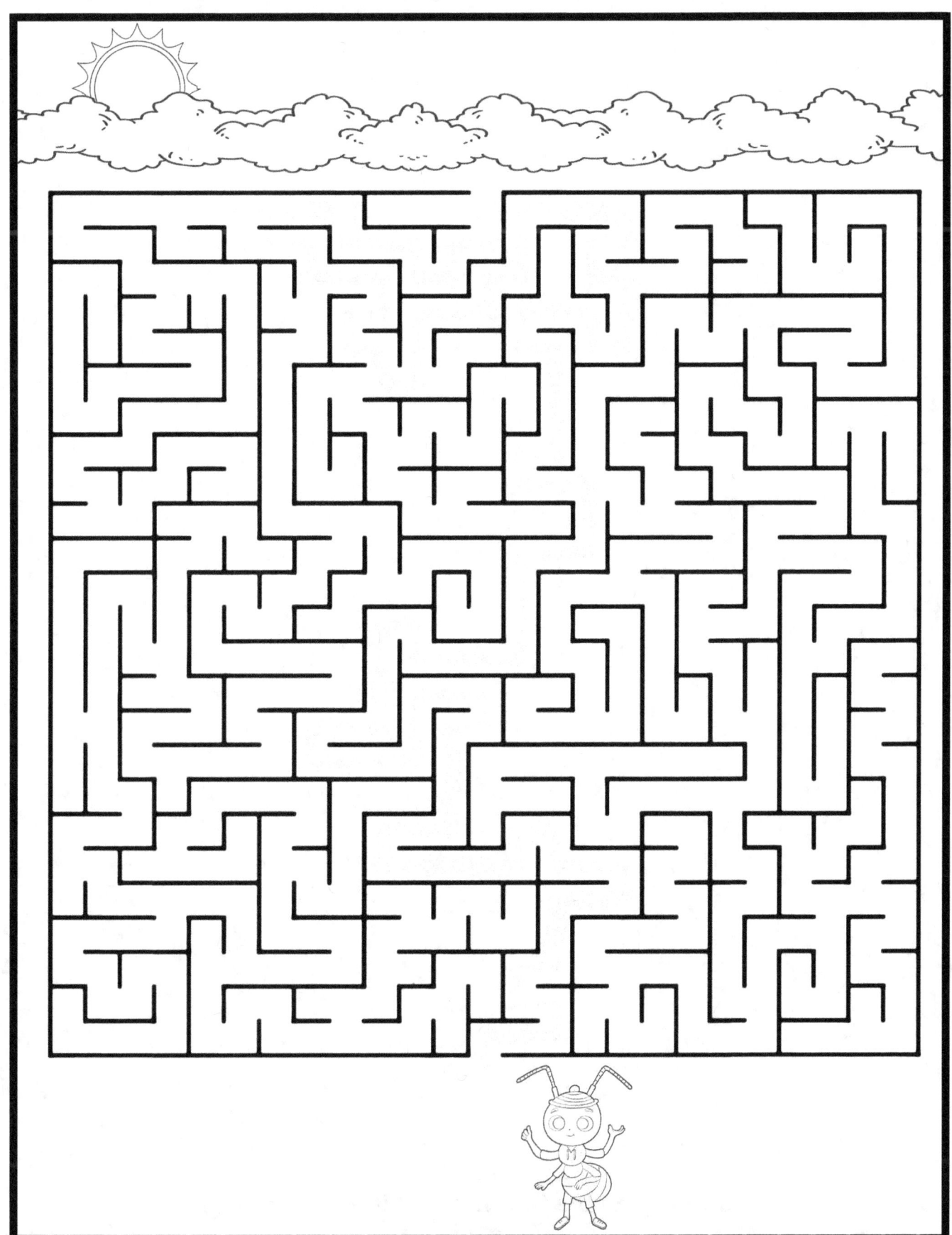

You can find the Solution to this maze on page 99.

Wanda wants to net a butterfly, but has lost her way. She needs your help to find the exit to use to leave the anthill.

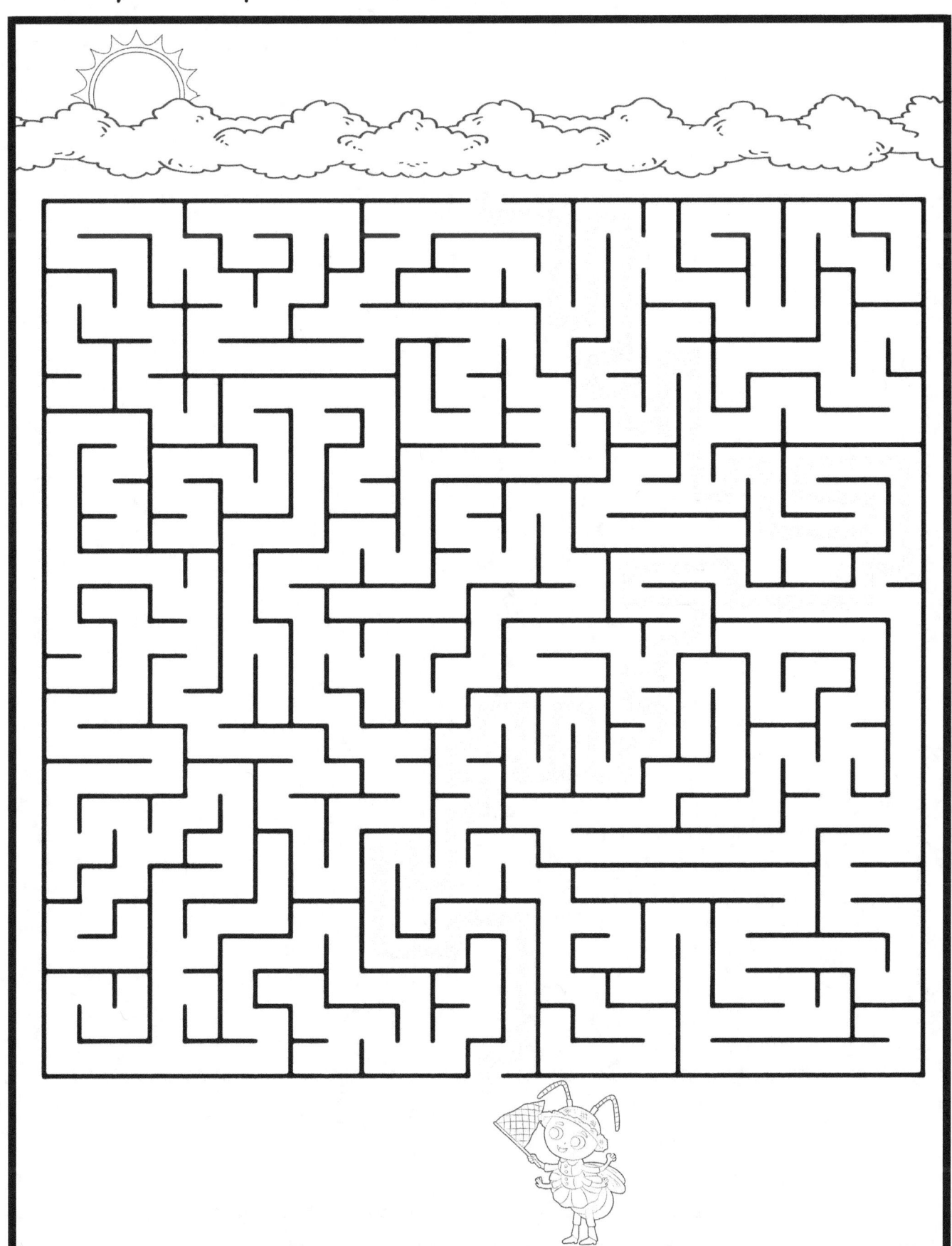

You can find the Solution to this maze on page 101.

Edgar is eager to go explore the nearby forest and needs your help to find the right path to take out of the anthill.

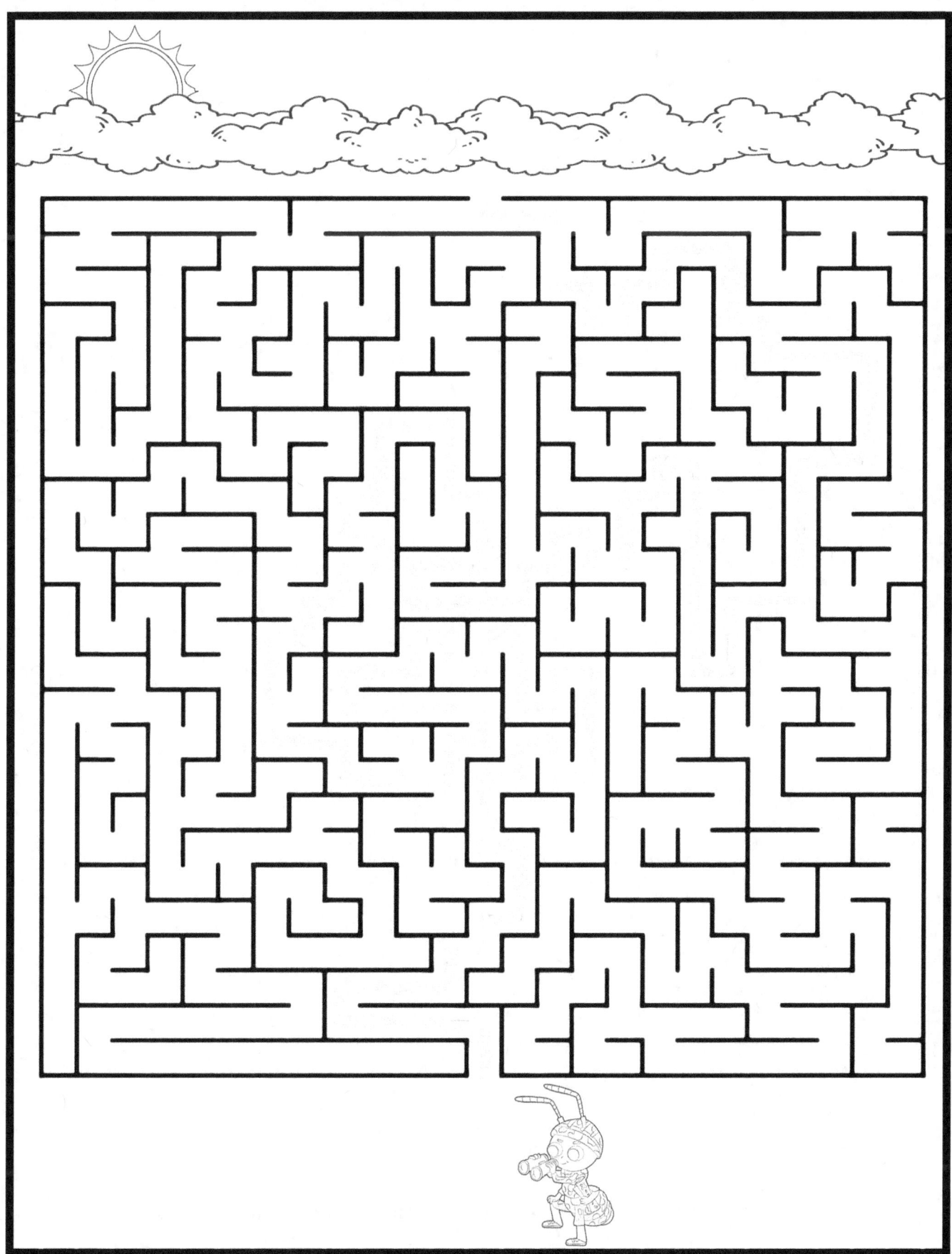

You can find the Solution to this maze on page 103.

Liam wants to practice walking on a tightrope and he could use your help get on the proper path to exit the anthill.

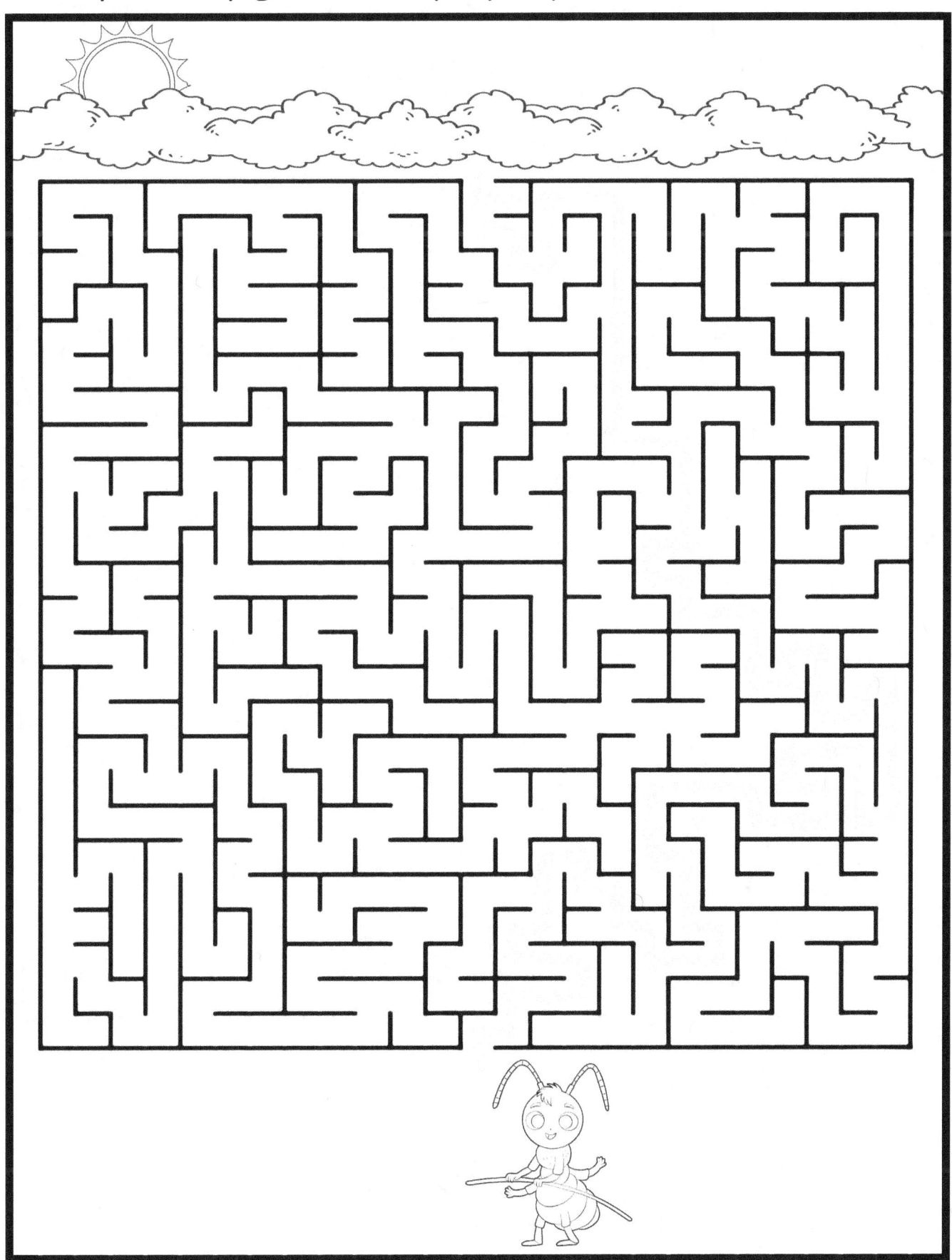

A group of fish is keeping **Izabel** company as she enjoys her river adventure floating along on her inner tube on the gentle waves in the water.

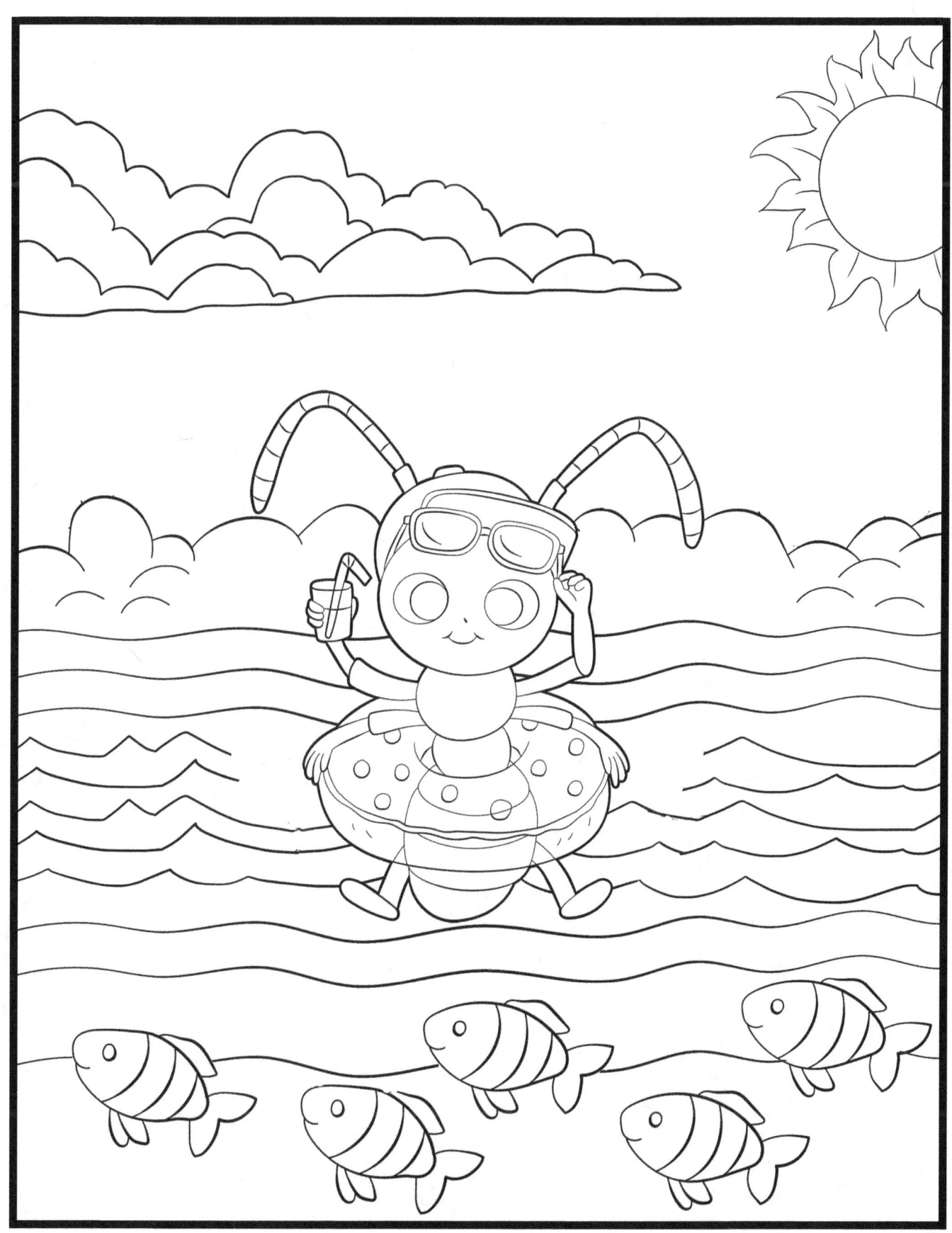

Izabel has found a quiet pond on the side of the river to rest and enjoy her refreshing cold drink before she heads back to her home in the anthill.

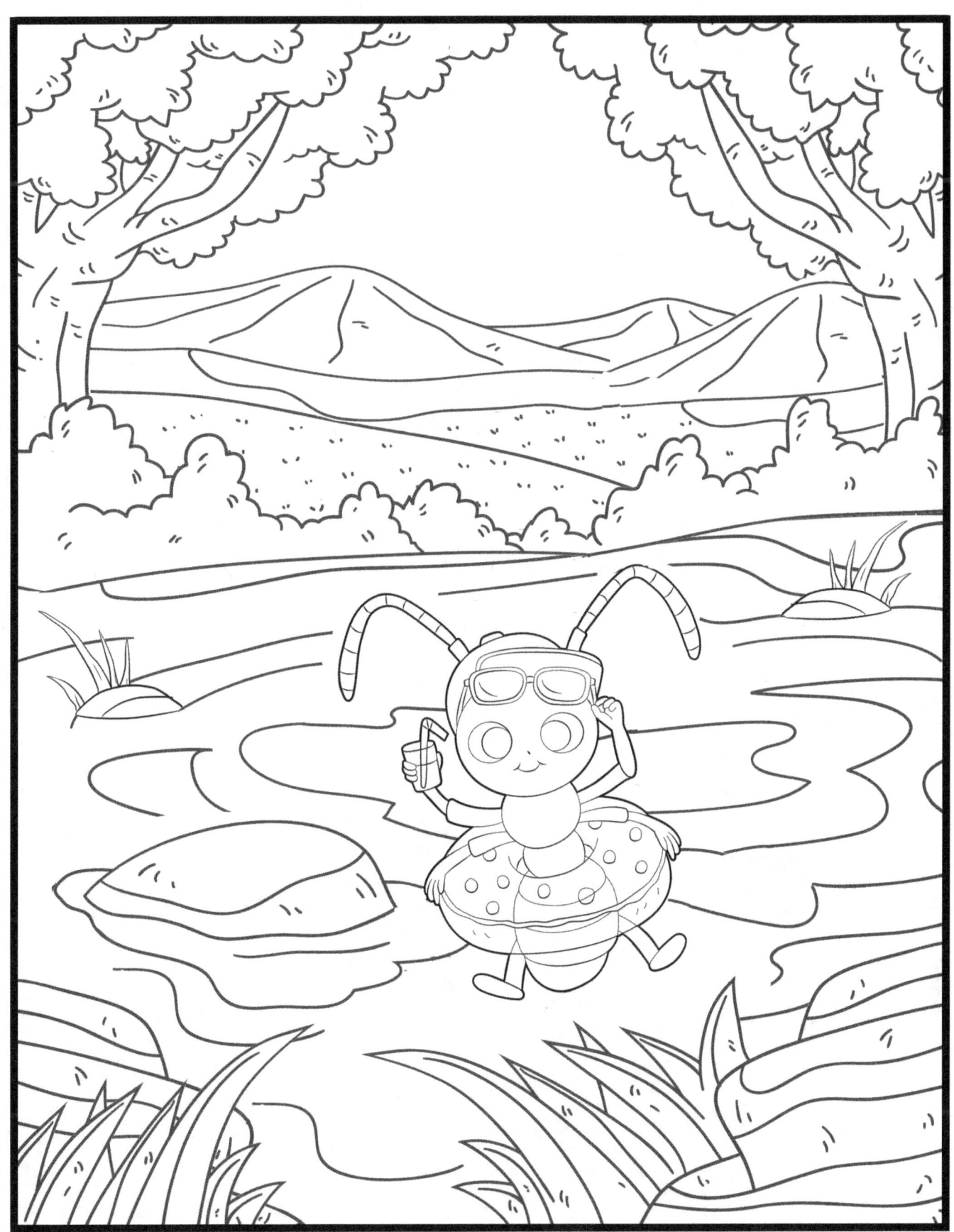

A flock of birds is following **Quinton** as he uses
a big leaf to fly around the forest. A beautiful
rainbow is arched over the mountains behind him.

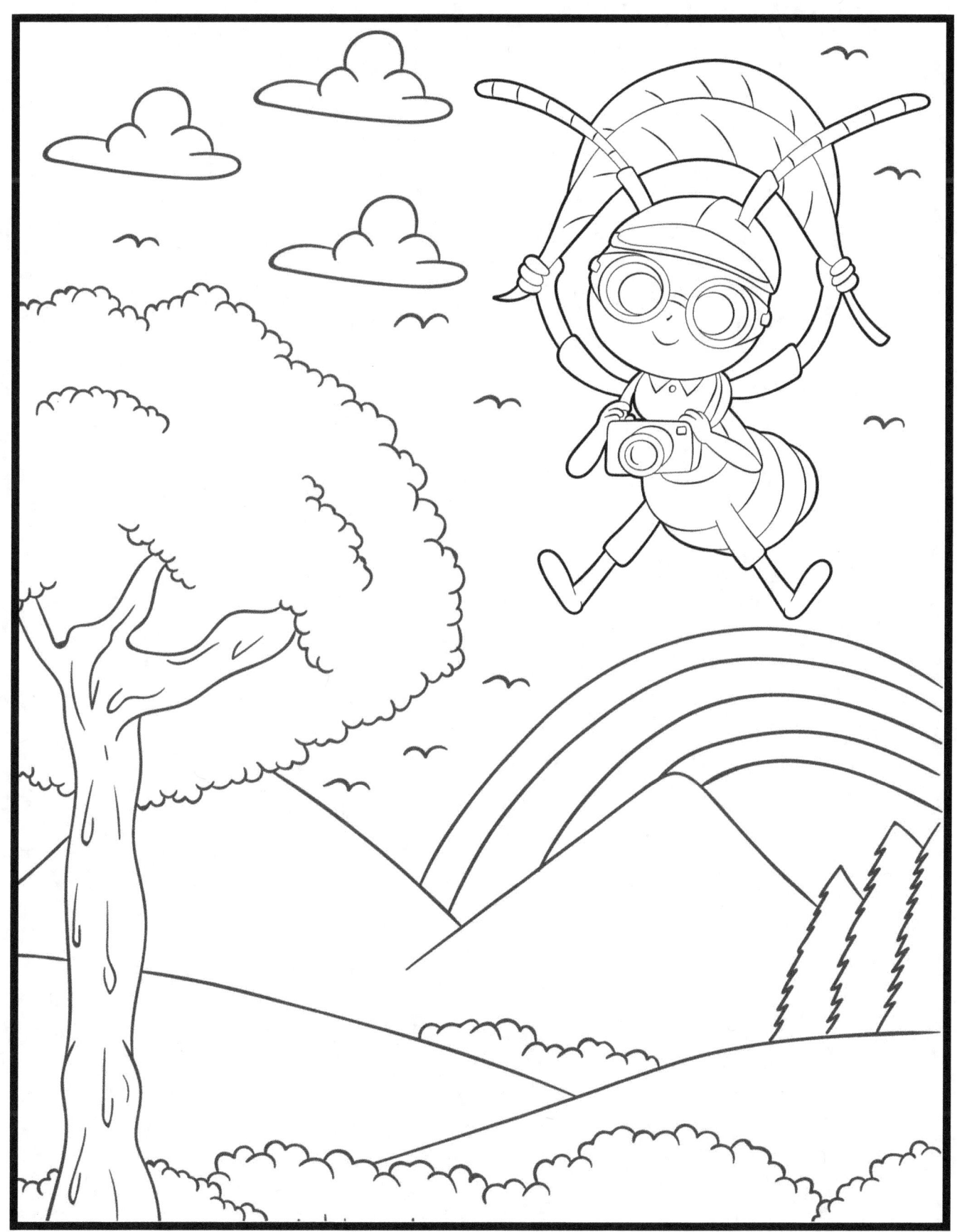

Quinton continued his flight around the forest. He took many photographs of the beautiful exotic flowers he saw in a field that he was flying over.

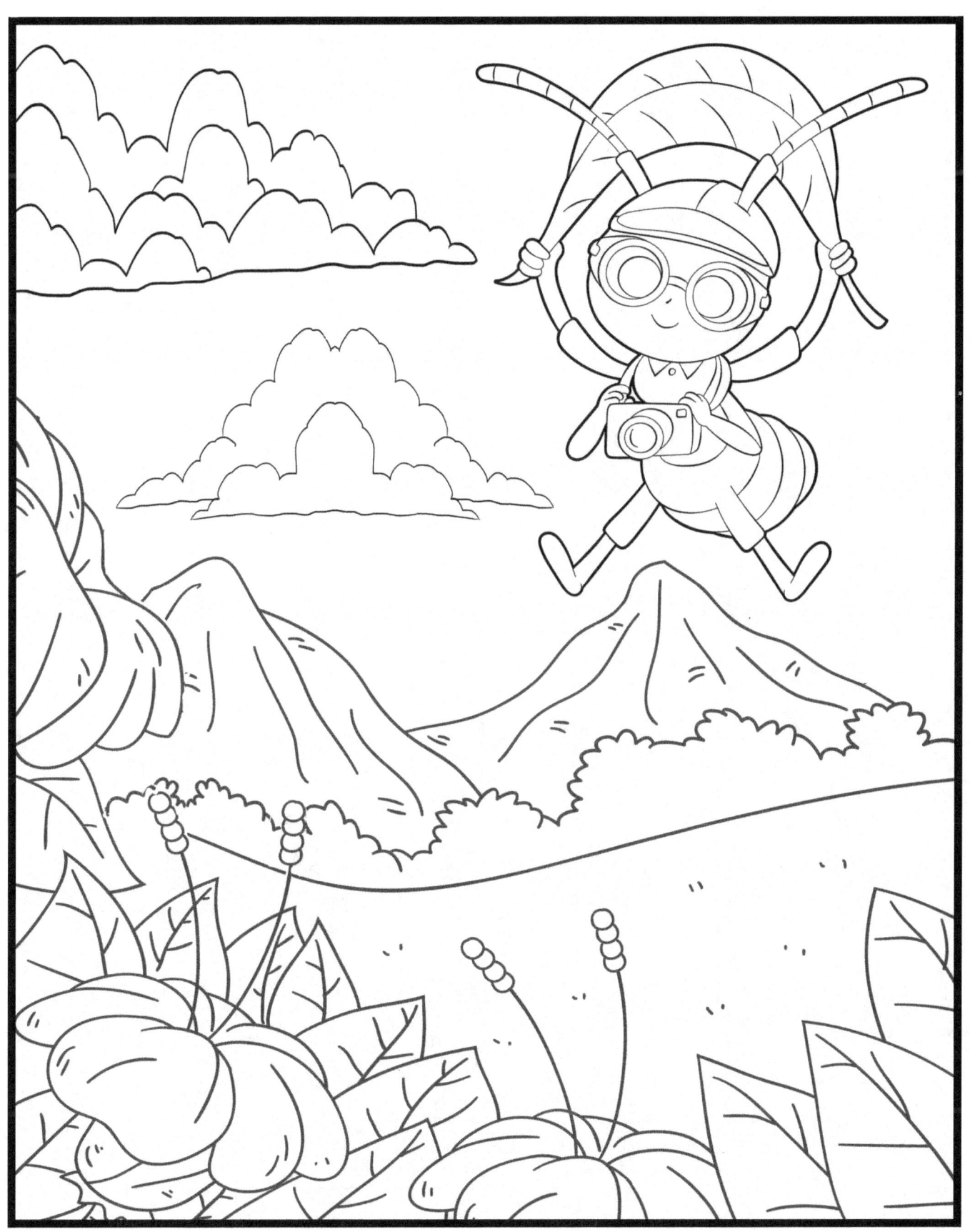

Yolandi loves to read! On this summer day, she used a hammock surrounded by lovely flowers and big leaves to sit on while reading her book.

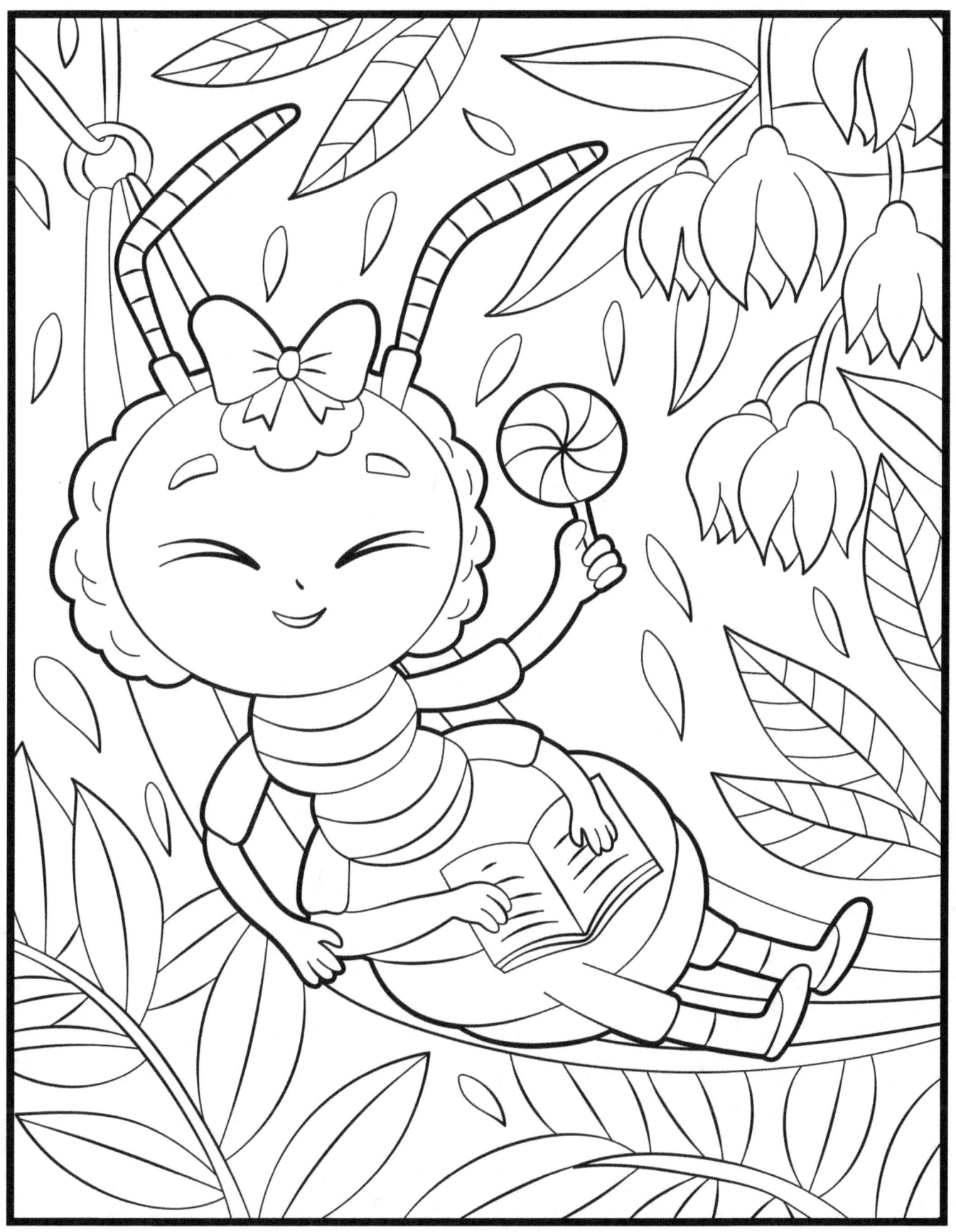

After **Yolandi** heard about some of the adventures her friends had, she traveled a little farther. She found a big branch, high above the forest, to sit on and read her book.

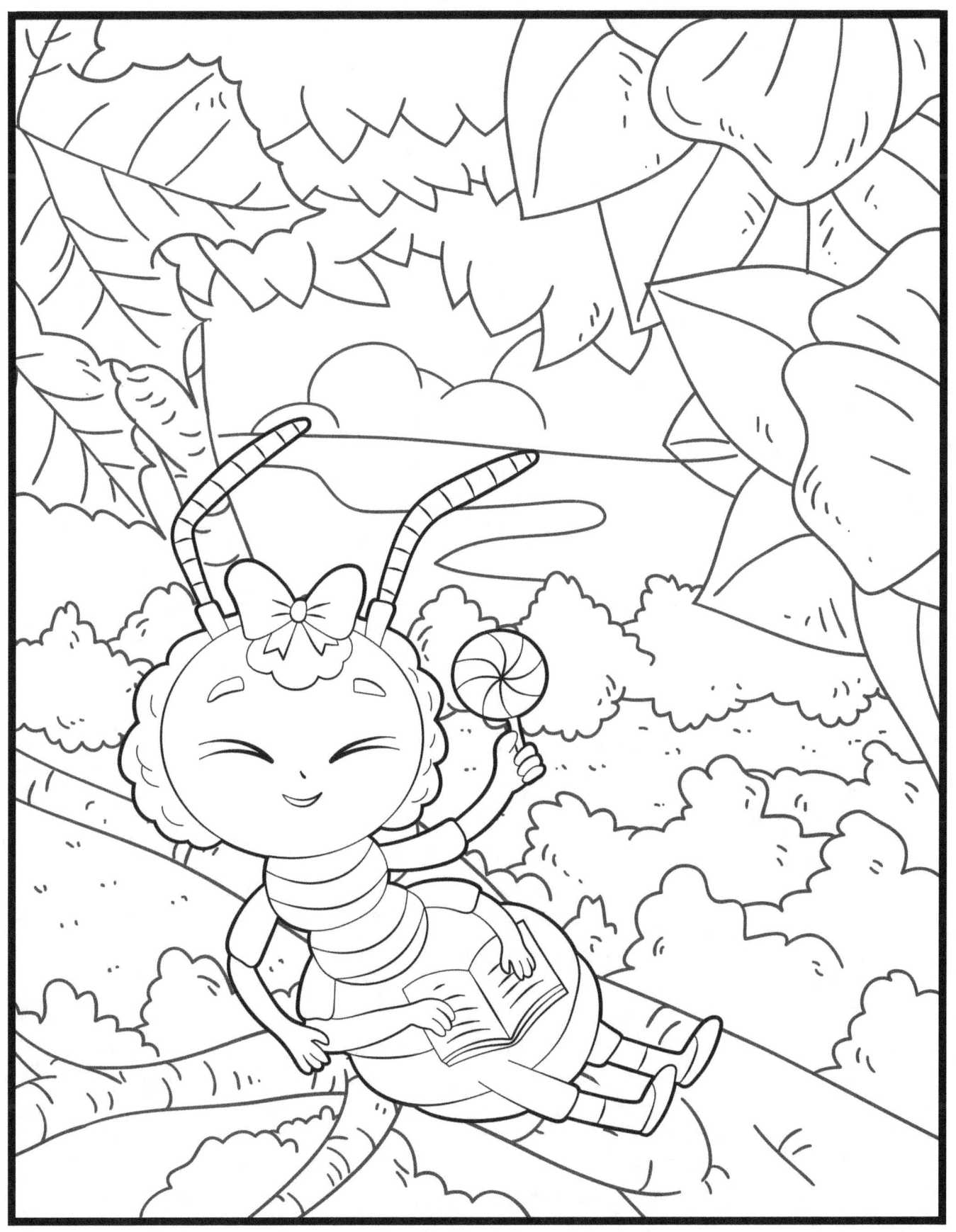

Xavier is the most adventurous ant in this book.
He became an astronaut and flew to the moon.

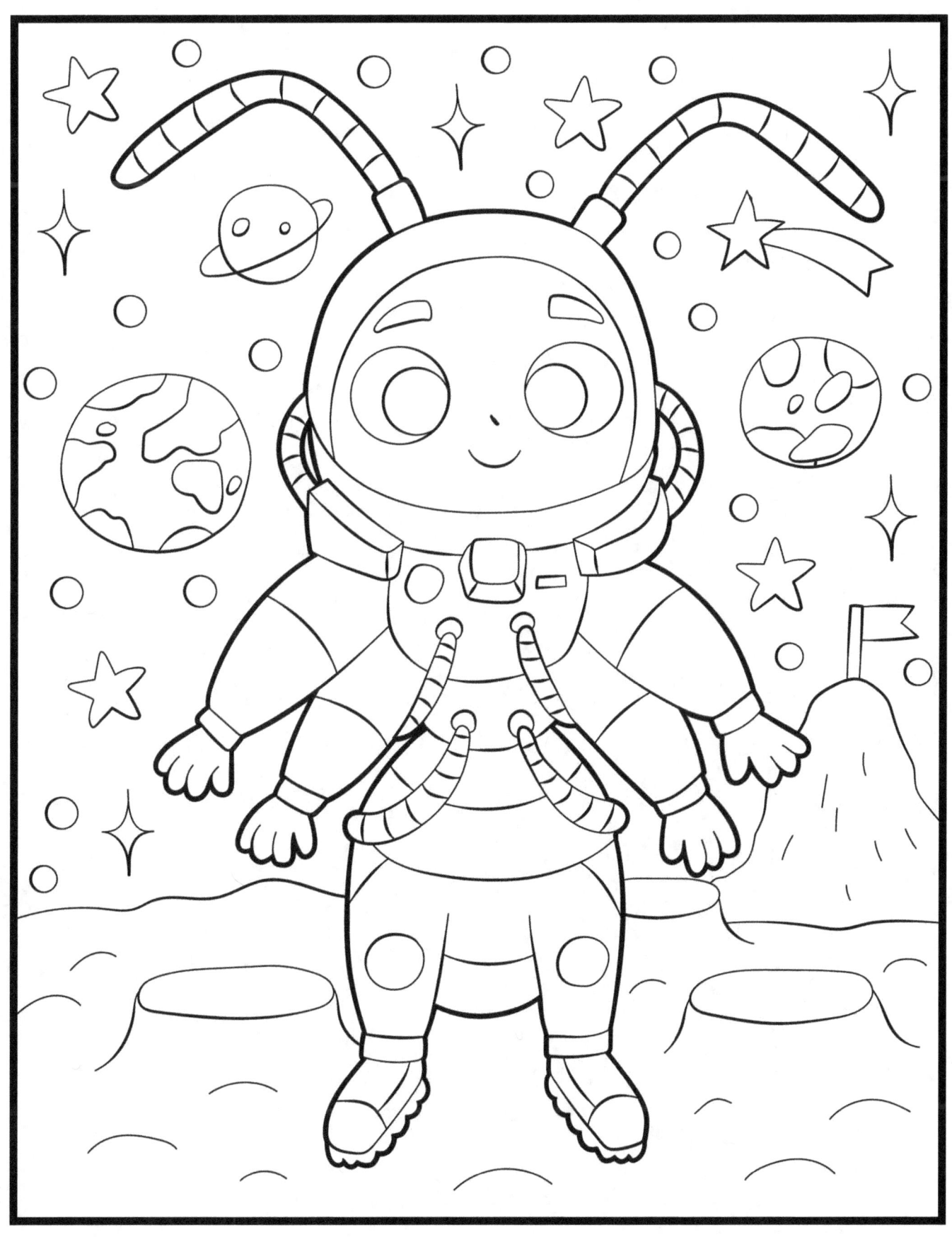

Now it is time for **Xavier** to stop his exploration of the moon and get back to his rocket ship to return to Earth. He will have some great stories to share with his friends.

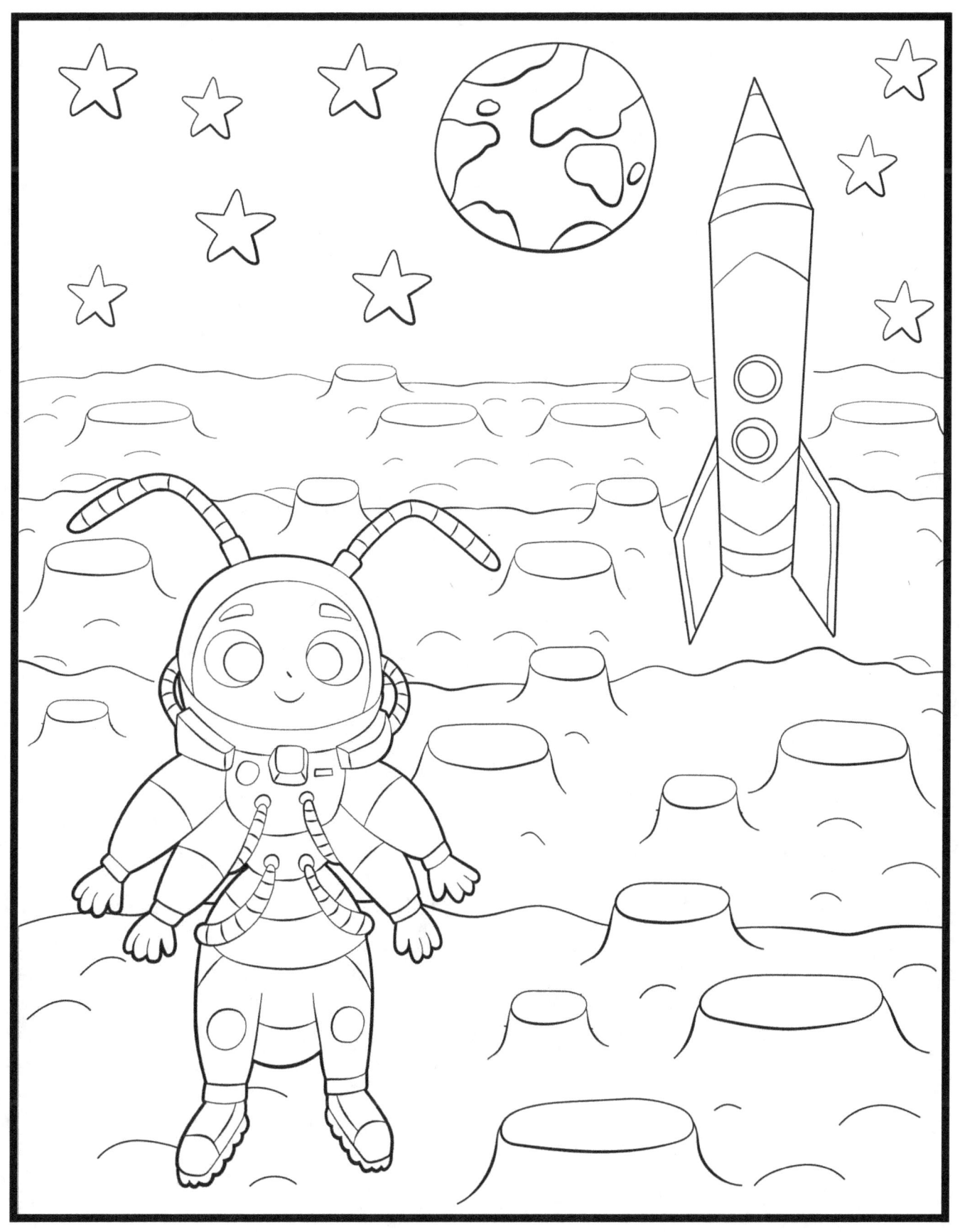

Adventurous Ants Names Word Search Puzzle.

Circle the words in the list when you find them in the square below.

Mark an X next to each word in the list when you find it.

Find the Solution on page 106.

__ ANNIE	__ LIAM	__ VICTOR
__ BERRI	__ MIKE	__ WANDA
__ CIARA	__ OLIVIA	__ XAVIER
__ EDGAR	__ PETER	__ YOLANDI
__ IZABEL	__ QUINTON	__ ZARA

V	B	M	N	S	X	Z	Q	A	P	V	A	D	R	S
E	T	I	W	A	O	P	R	Y	E	I	N	N	A	N
G	Z	A	V	X	C	A	F	O	T	K	Z	X	G	W
B	V	I	B	P	I	Z	A	B	E	L	S	I	D	B
S	E	P	E	C	L	Y	Z	A	R	J	T	F	E	L
R	M	R	T	A	C	Q	U	D	F	F	E	K	I	M
I	E	G	R	K	S	I	Y	O	M	G	L	E	D	J
Y	X	A	N	I	L	C	J	Q	R	I	Z	A	W	X
K	Z	F	I	D	V	G	U	I	D	N	A	L	O	Y
B	O	S	N	T	M	I	B	E	T	Y	N	O	L	K
V	M	J	Z	W	N	L	C	X	P	O	X	V	I	G
D	V	C	Y	T	P	I	C	T	U	Q	J	L	V	E
T	A	Q	O	F	W	A	S	E	O	K	G	D	I	C
W	A	N	D	A	L	M	L	I	N	R	F	B	A	P
G	Z	J	P	M	X	D	O	T	A	W	E	S	K	N

Adventurous Ants Glossary Word Search Puzzle.

Circle the words in the list when you find them in the square below.

Mark an X next to each word in the list when you find it.

Find the Solution on page 107.

__ **APPLE**
__ **ASTRONAUT**
__ **BEEHIVE**
__ **BUTTERFLY**
__ **BIRTHDAY**

__ **CASTLE**
__ **CEREMONY**
__ **FRIENDS**
__ **FLOWERS**
__ **HARVEST**

__ **JUNGLE**
__ **MACHETE**
__ **PLANTING**
__ **SHOVEL**
__ **WATERMELON**

M	L	P	O	Z	S	R	T	A	J	F	L	H	Q	U
I	C	W	E	C	V	Y	L	F	R	E	T	T	U	B
E	V	I	H	E	E	B	D	G	E	Z	O	R	E	I
A	L	S	E	L	G	N	U	J	Z	W	L	T	A	R
L	P	T	R	P	I	S	J	Z	F	V	E	W	X	T
T	M	V	S	P	M	R	I	G	L	K	V	D	G	H
U	H	S	W	A	T	E	R	M	E	L	O	N	R	D
A	H	O	A	T	C	W	D	E	A	Z	H	S	F	A
N	V	A	H	E	S	O	Z	Z	G	C	S	D	H	Y
O	D	P	R	X	R	L	M	H	C	V	H	N	P	S
R	Z	L	F	V	I	F	R	A	D	Z	P	E	J	V
T	S	T	G	C	E	R	E	M	O	N	Y	I	T	I
S	C	E	W	K	J	S	V	X	M	O	C	R	A	E
A	D	R	Z	G	N	I	T	N	A	L	P	F	S	T
P	I	V	Z	S	T	P	G	L	E	F	L	O	W	M

Connect the dots to discover what **Peter** is doing. Color the surrounding design to give him a colorful border.

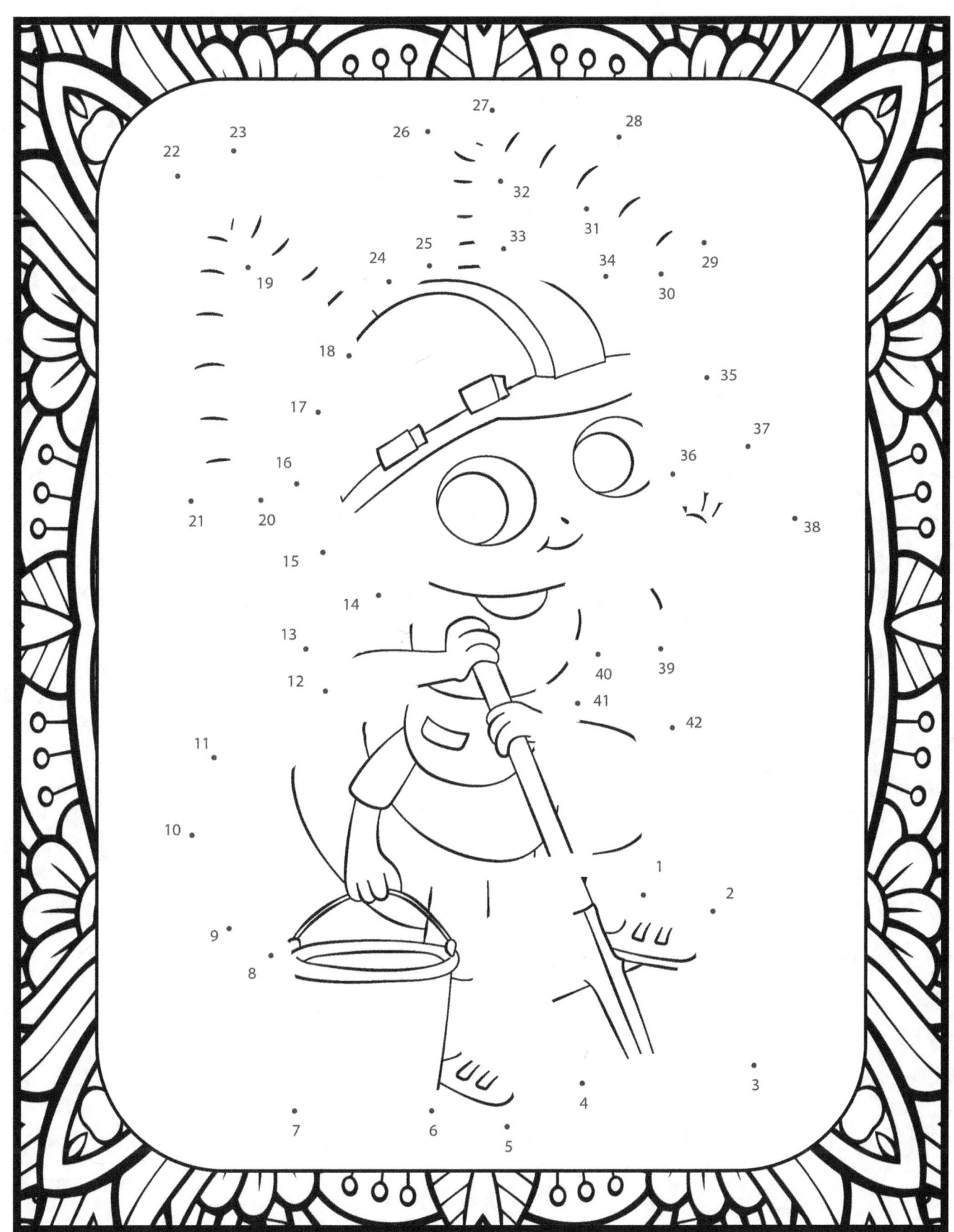

Connect the dots to discover what **Gale** is doing. Color the surrounding design to give her a colorful border.

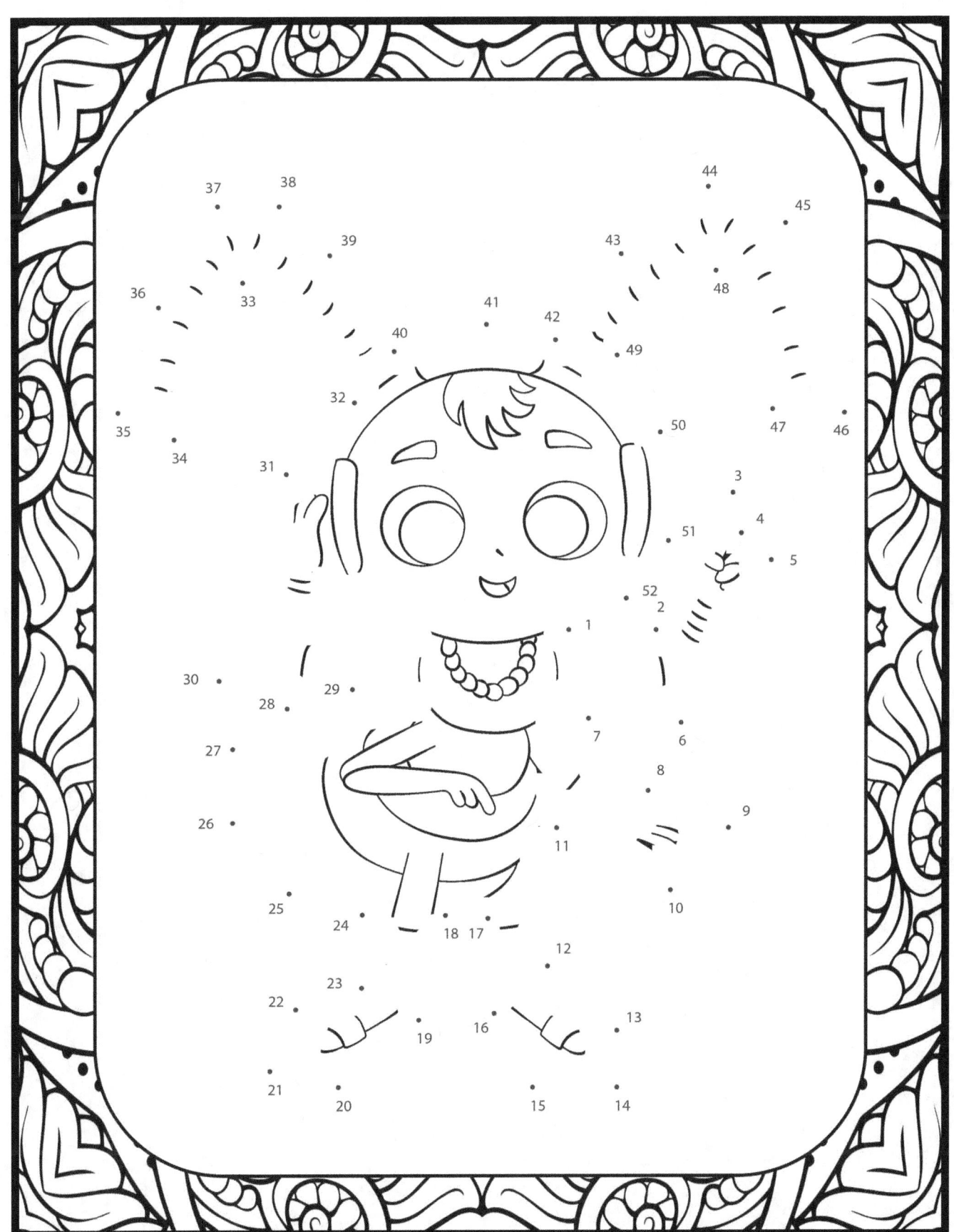

Connect the dots to discover what **Quinton** is doing. Color the surrounding design to give him a colorful border.

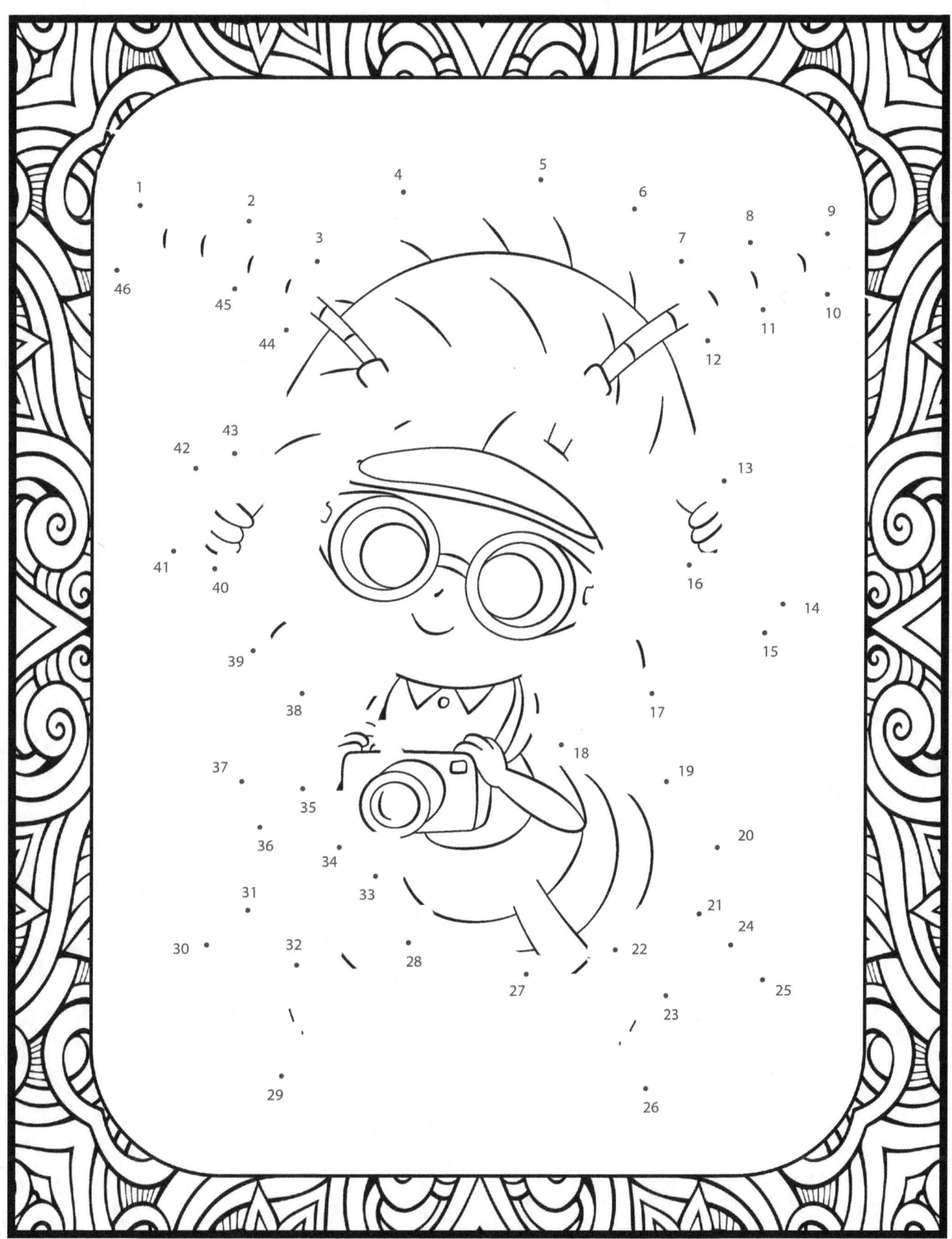

Connect the dots to discover what **Olivia** is doing. Color the surrounding design to give her a colorful border.

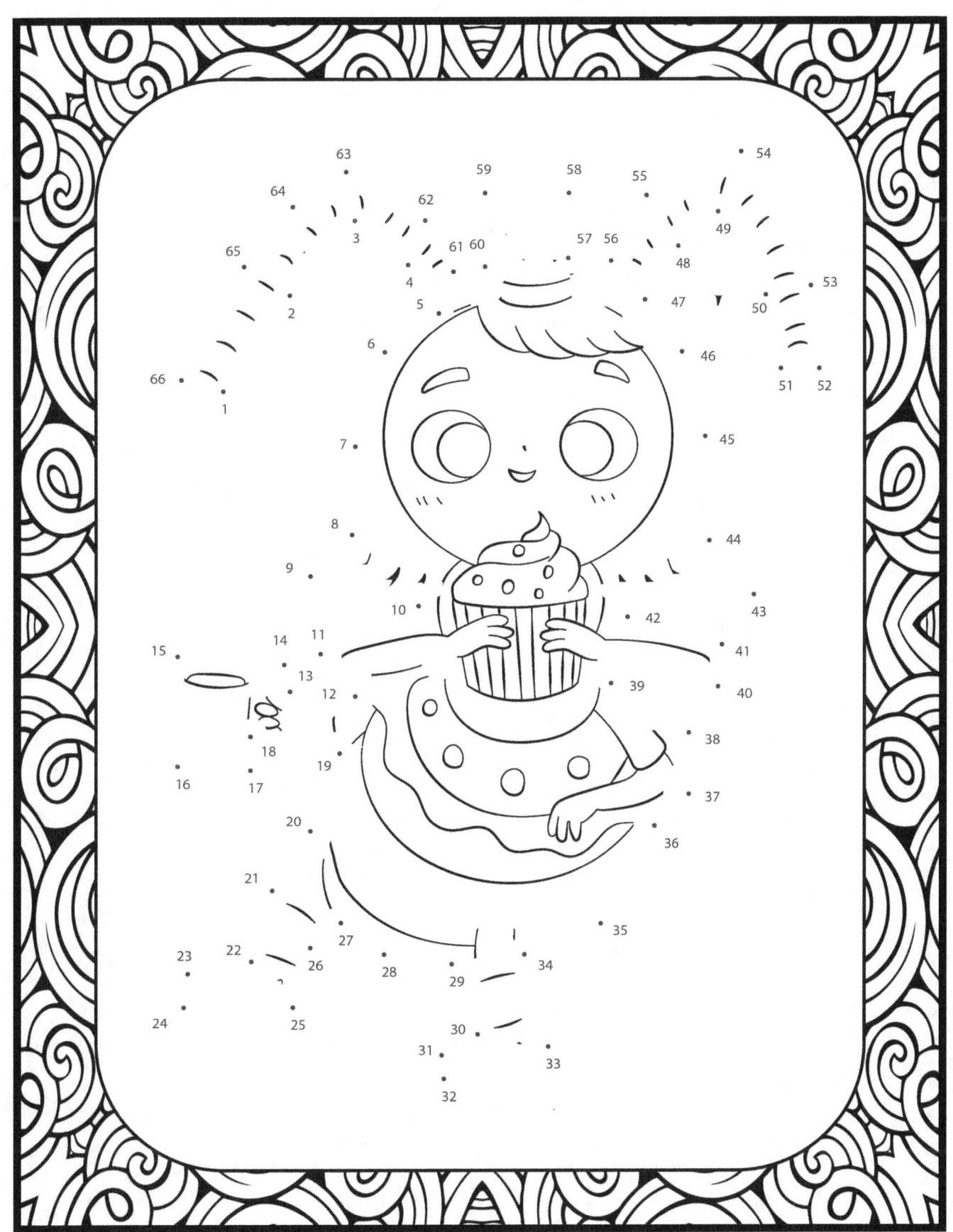

Connect the dots to discover what **Xavier** is doing. Color the surrounding design to give him a colorful border.

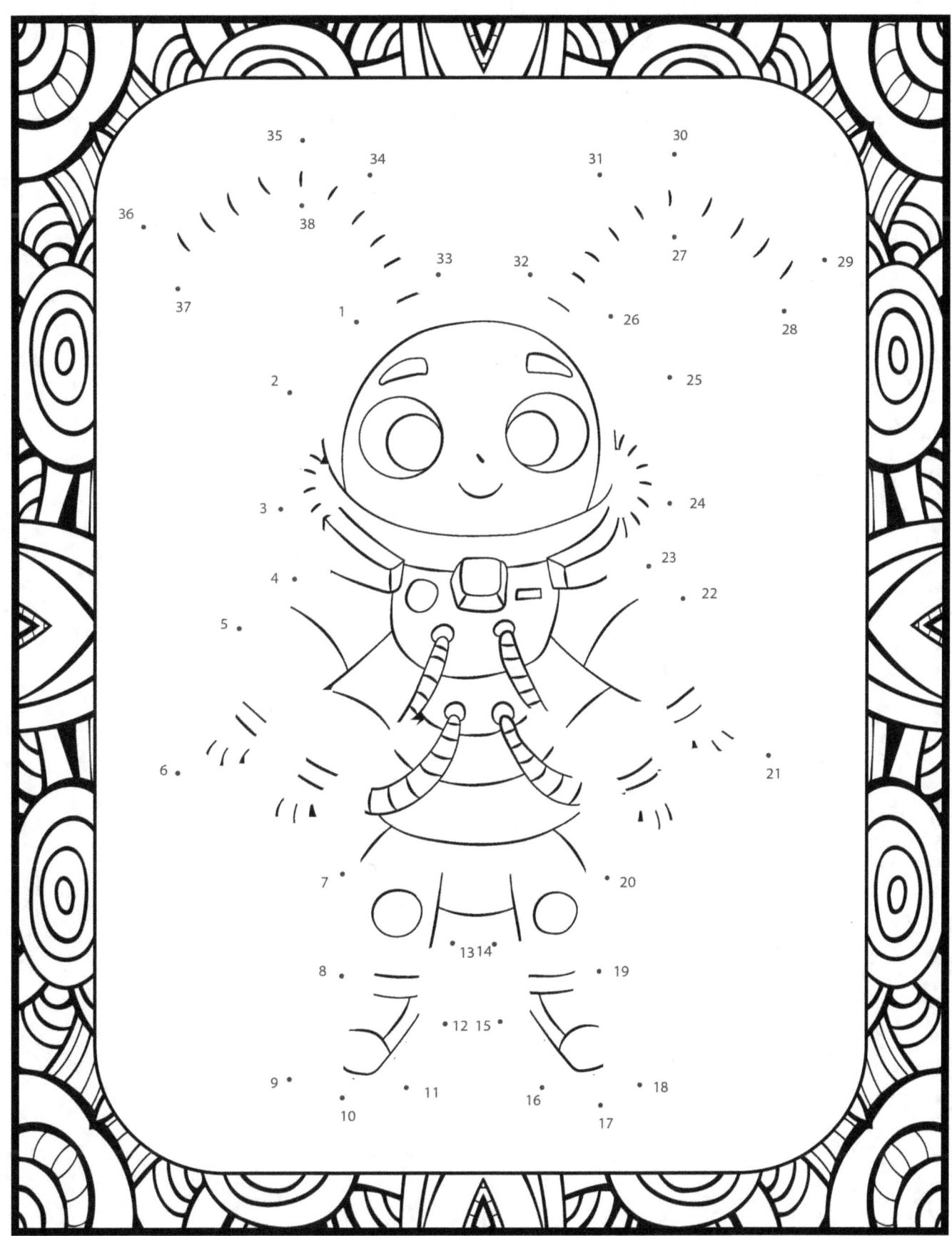

Connect the dots to discover what **Izabel** is doing. Color the surrounding design to give her a colorful border.

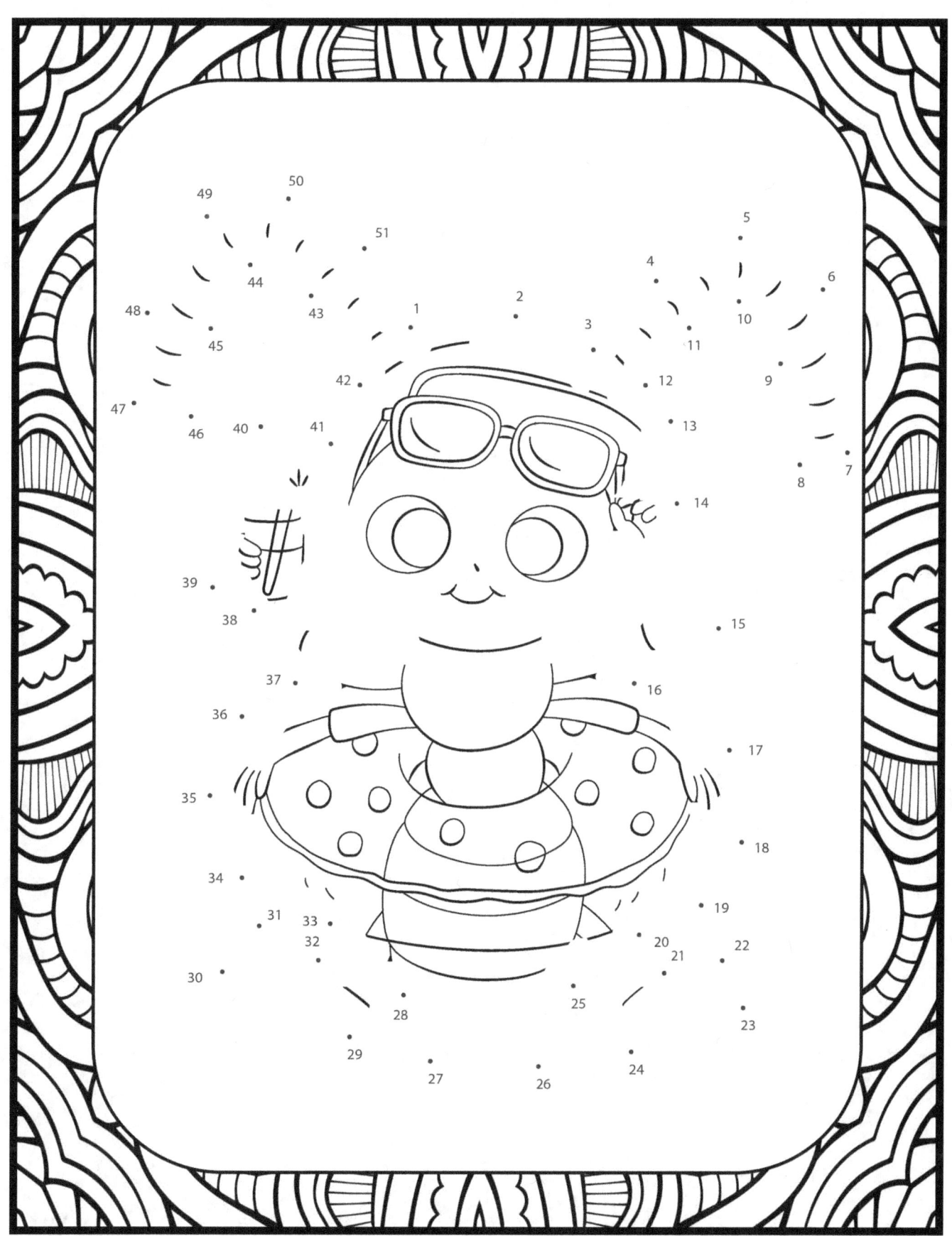

Connect the dots to discover what **Victor** is doing. Color the surrounding design to give him a colorful border.

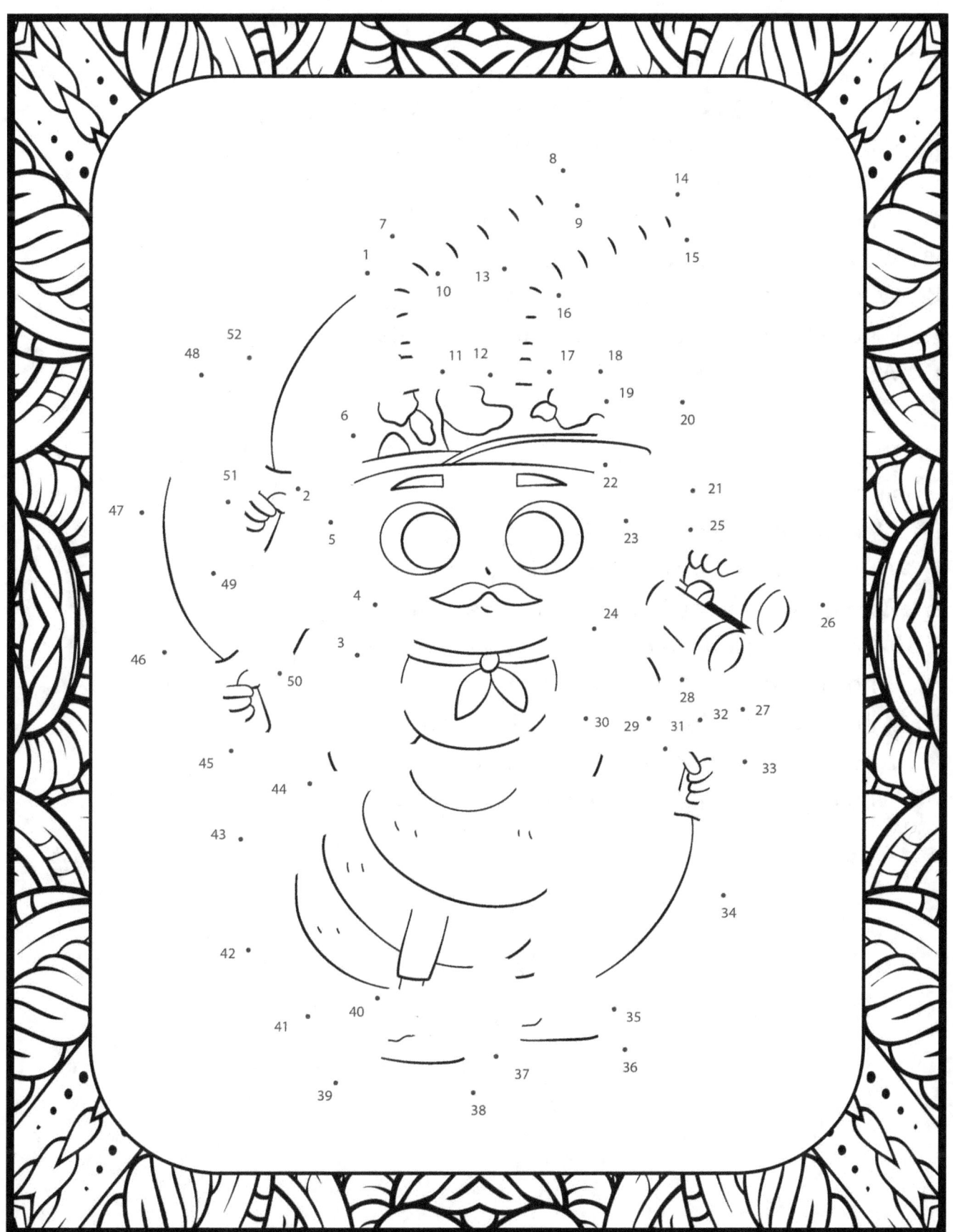

Clues for the Adventurous Ants
Names Crossword Puzzle.

ACROSS

4. Who is bringing a cake to a birthday celebration? _____

5. Who is carrying machetes to explore the jungle? _____

8. Who is using binoculars to watch bees and butterflies? _____

9. Who is dancing around a fire in a mountain valley? _____

11. Who is practicing walking on a tightwire?_____

12. Who is reading a book on a hammock? _____

15. Who is bringing a cupcake to a birthday celebration? _____

16. Who is picking apples by a barn? _____

DOWN

1. Who traveled to the moon? _____

2. Who planted a lot of flowers in his garden? _____

3. Who is enjoying eating slices of a watermelon? _____

6. Who went looking to capture butterflies in a net? _____

7. Who floated down a river in an inner tube? _____

10. Who used a big leaf to fly around the forest? _____

13. Who is on a path to visit a castle in the sky? _____

14. Who is playing disco music? _____

Adventurous Ants Names Crossword Puzzle.
Solution on page 109.

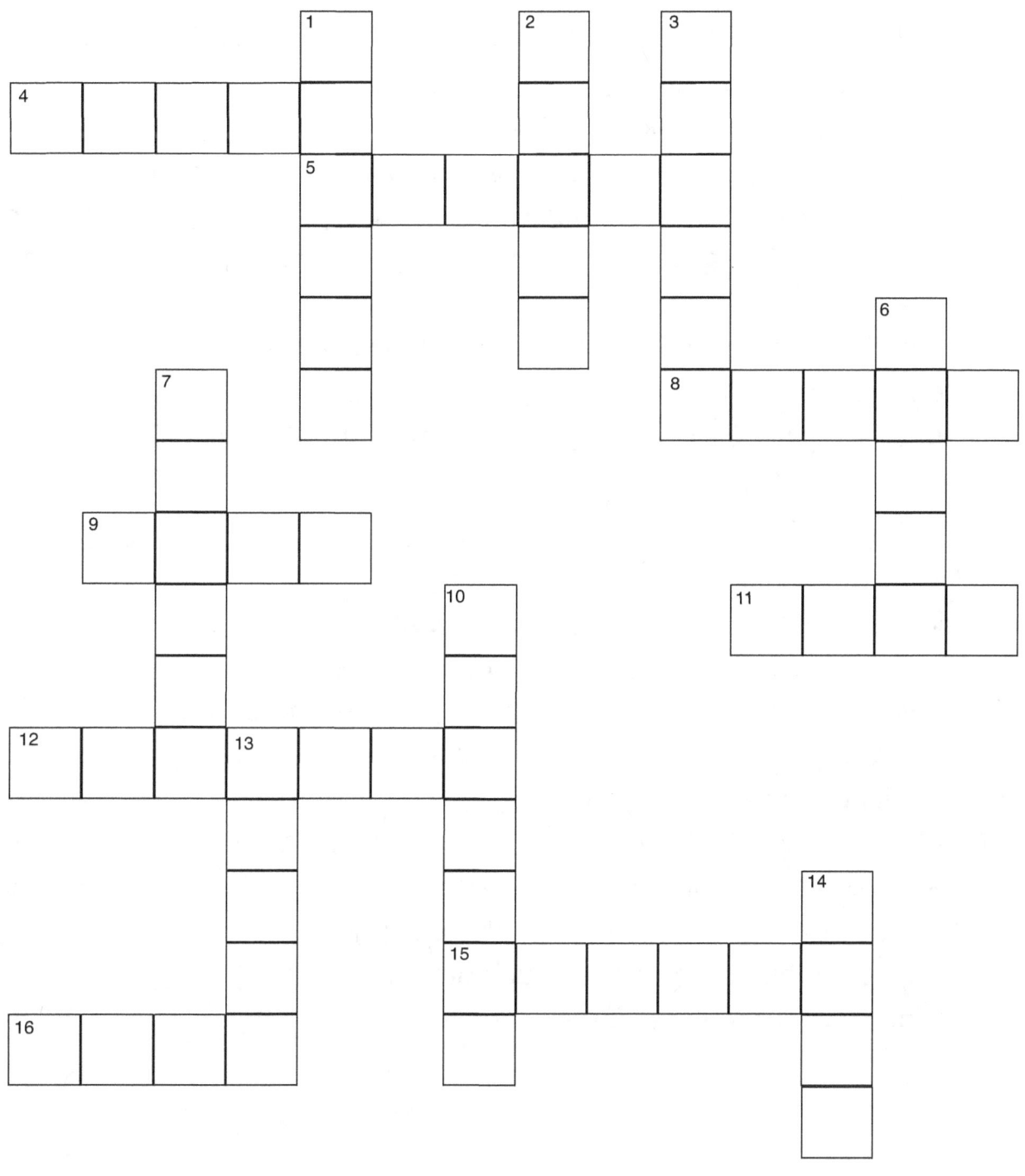

Clues for the Adventurous Ants
Glossary Word Crossword Puzzle.

ACROSS

2. Xavier is an _____ who went into outer space in a rocket.
4. Xavier traveled to the _____ on his big adventure.
5. Olivia brought a cupcake to a field of flowers for her _____.
7. Liam used a _____ to balance himself on a tightrope.
8. Annie dressed as a fairy princess went to a _____ in the night sky.
10. Izabel traveled in an inner tube to _____ down a river.
11. Peter was busy _____ flowers on a sunny day.
13. Edgar took a map of the _____ to find a bee hive.
16. Berri enjoyed eating slices of a _____.
19. Ciara brought a Cake to _____ her birthday with Olivia.

DOWN

1. Victor carried a _____ on his adventure in a jungle.
2. Mike went to pick _____ on a tree near a barn.
3. A rainbow is arched over the _____ behind Quinton.
6. Yolandi enjoyed _____ a book in a hammock.
9. Wanda left the anthill carrying a _____ net.
12. Peter spent a day planting _____ in his garden.
14. Zara was dancing around a fire near a _____ in a mountain valley.
15. Mike stood on hay _____ to pick apples.
17. Edgar used his binoculars to watch butterflies and _____.
18. Quinton flew around the forest using a big _____.

Solution for the Adventurous Ants
Glossary Word Crossword Puzzle on page 111.

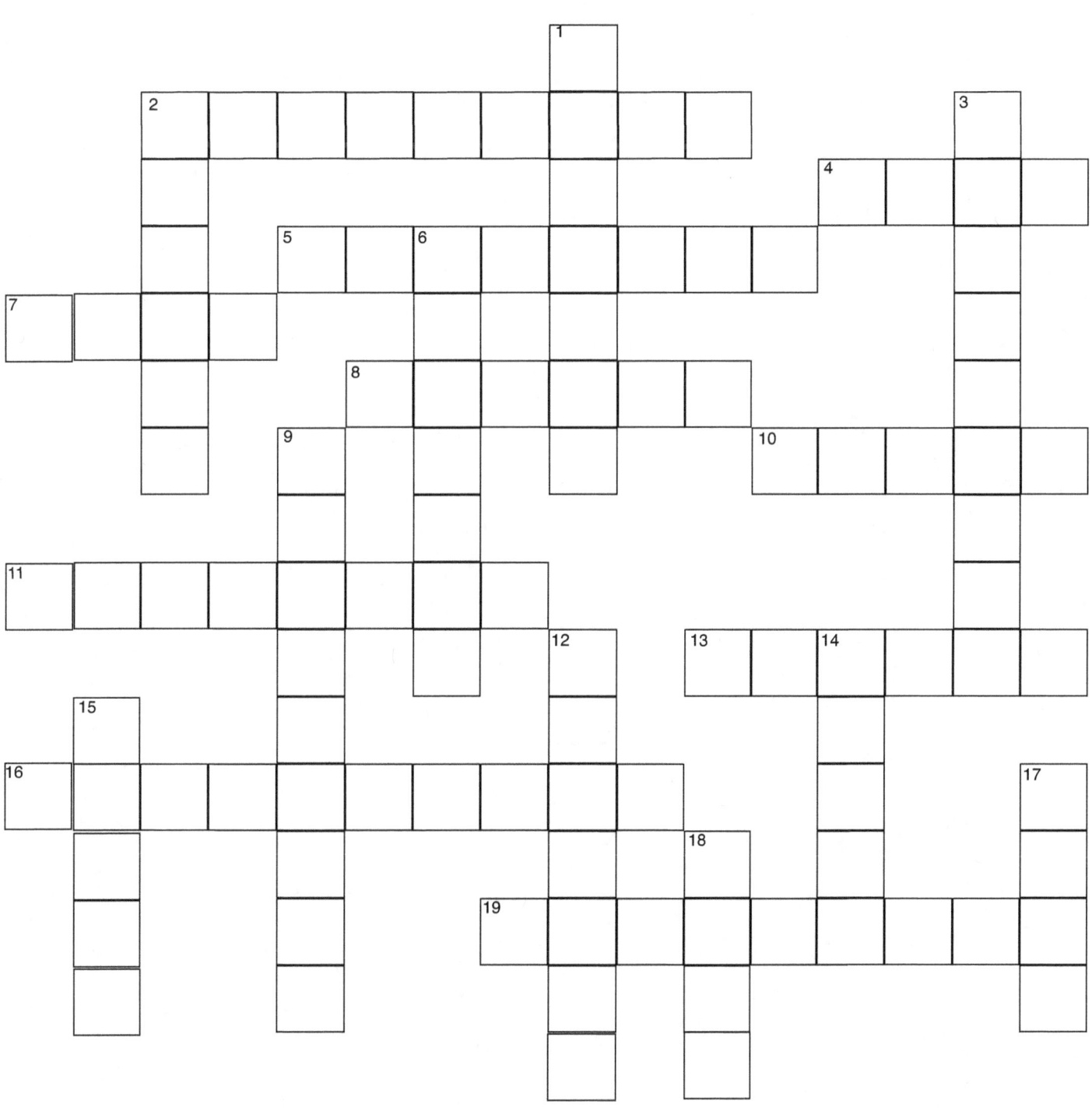

Design to Color.

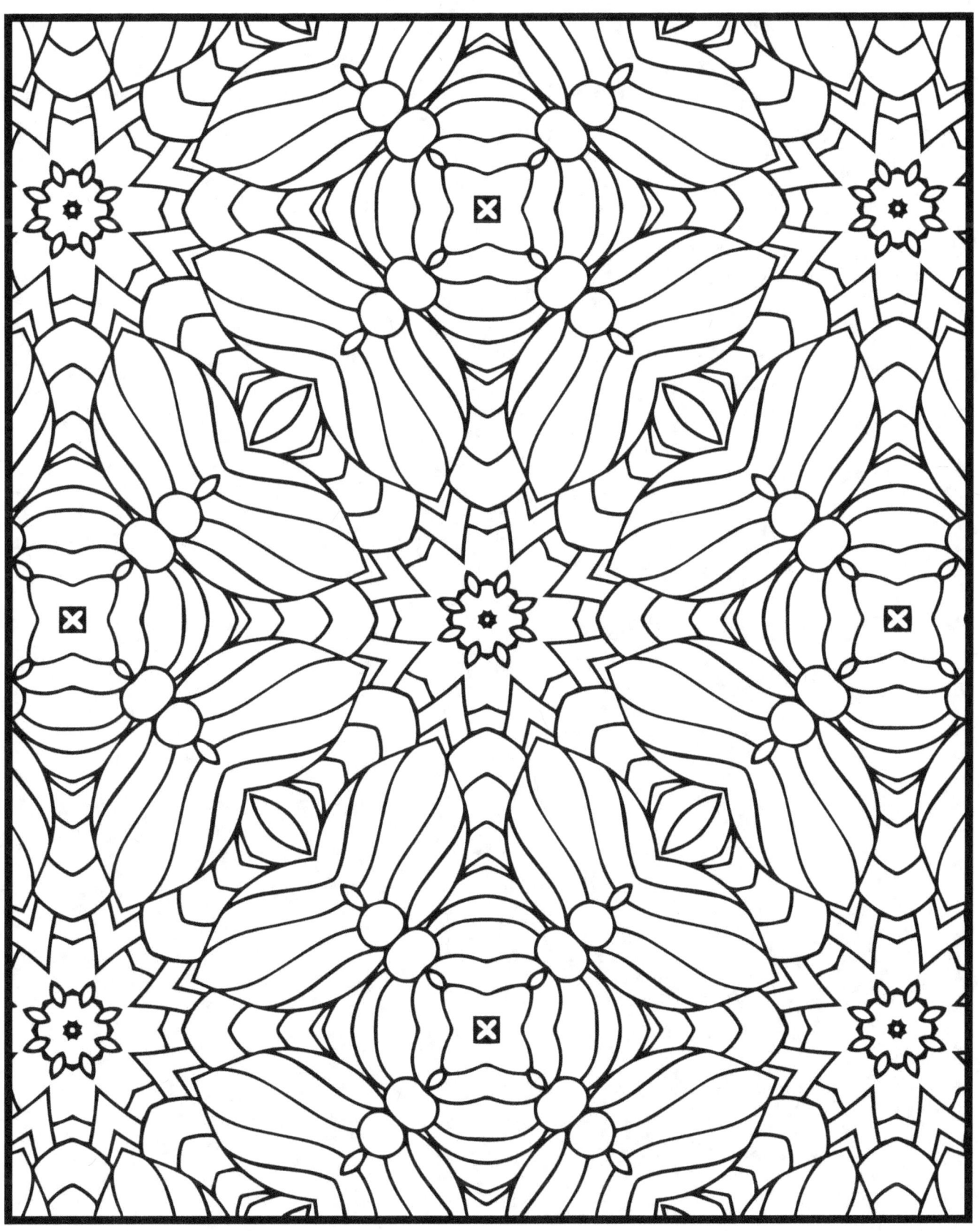

Design to Color.

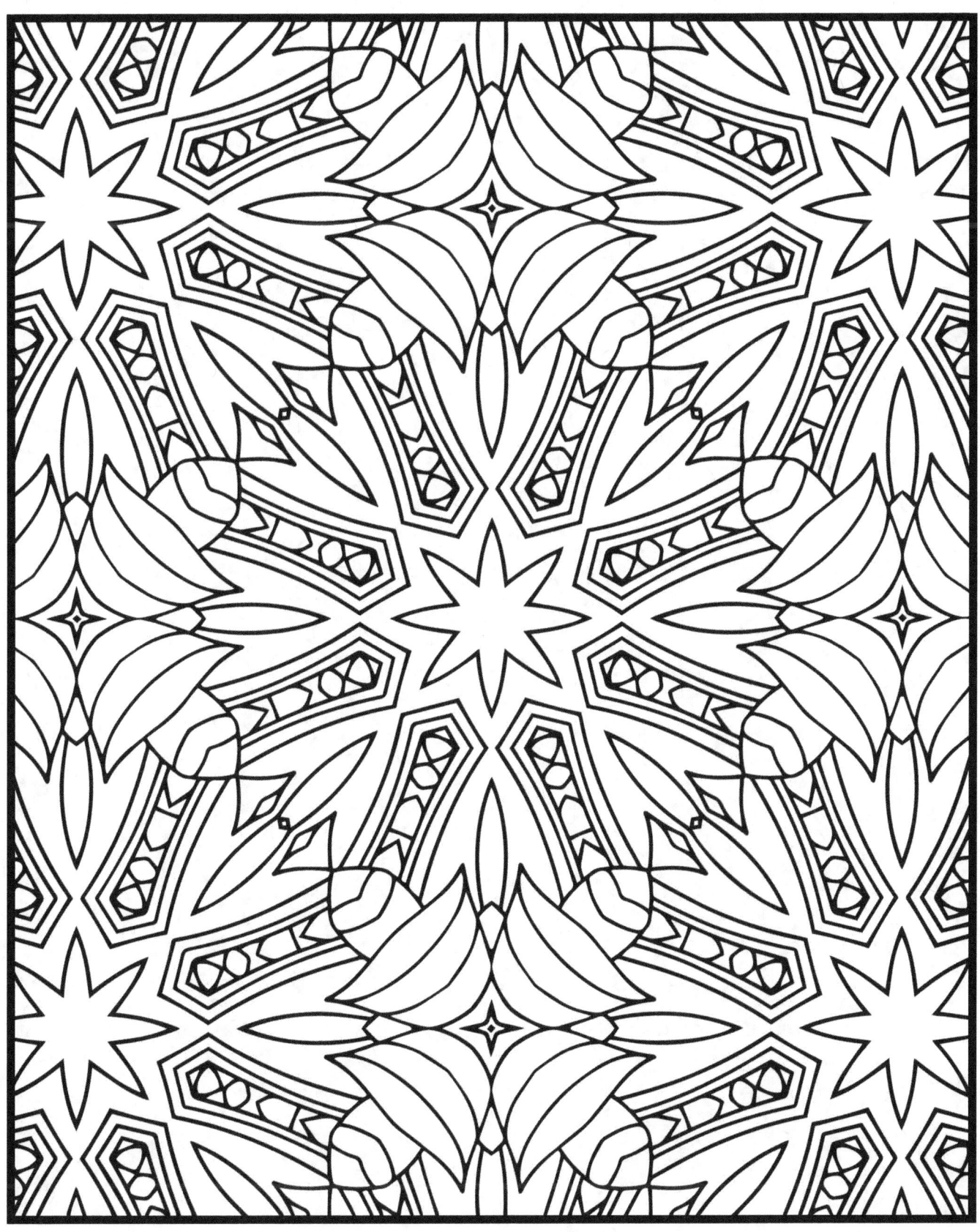

Design to Color.

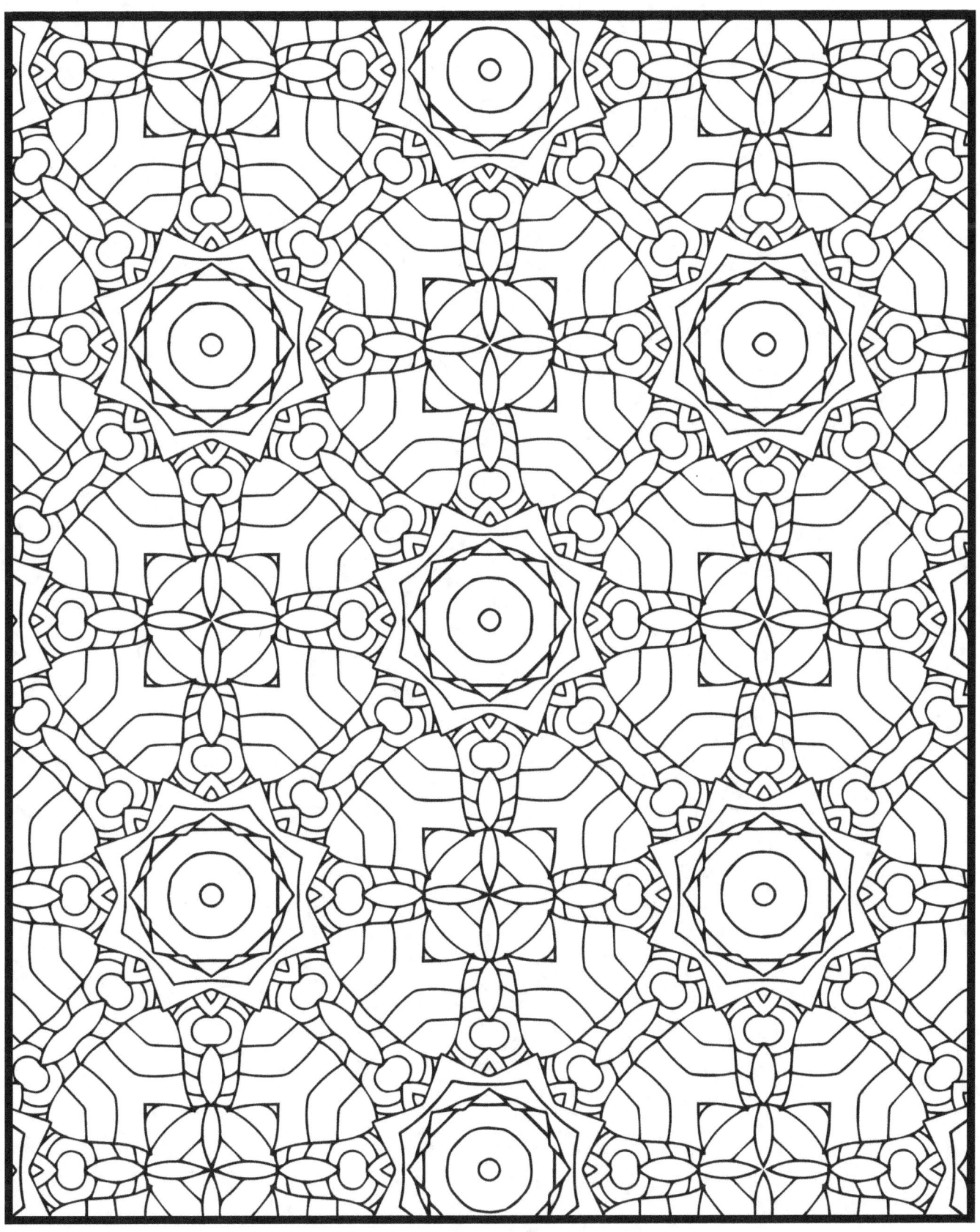

Design to Color.

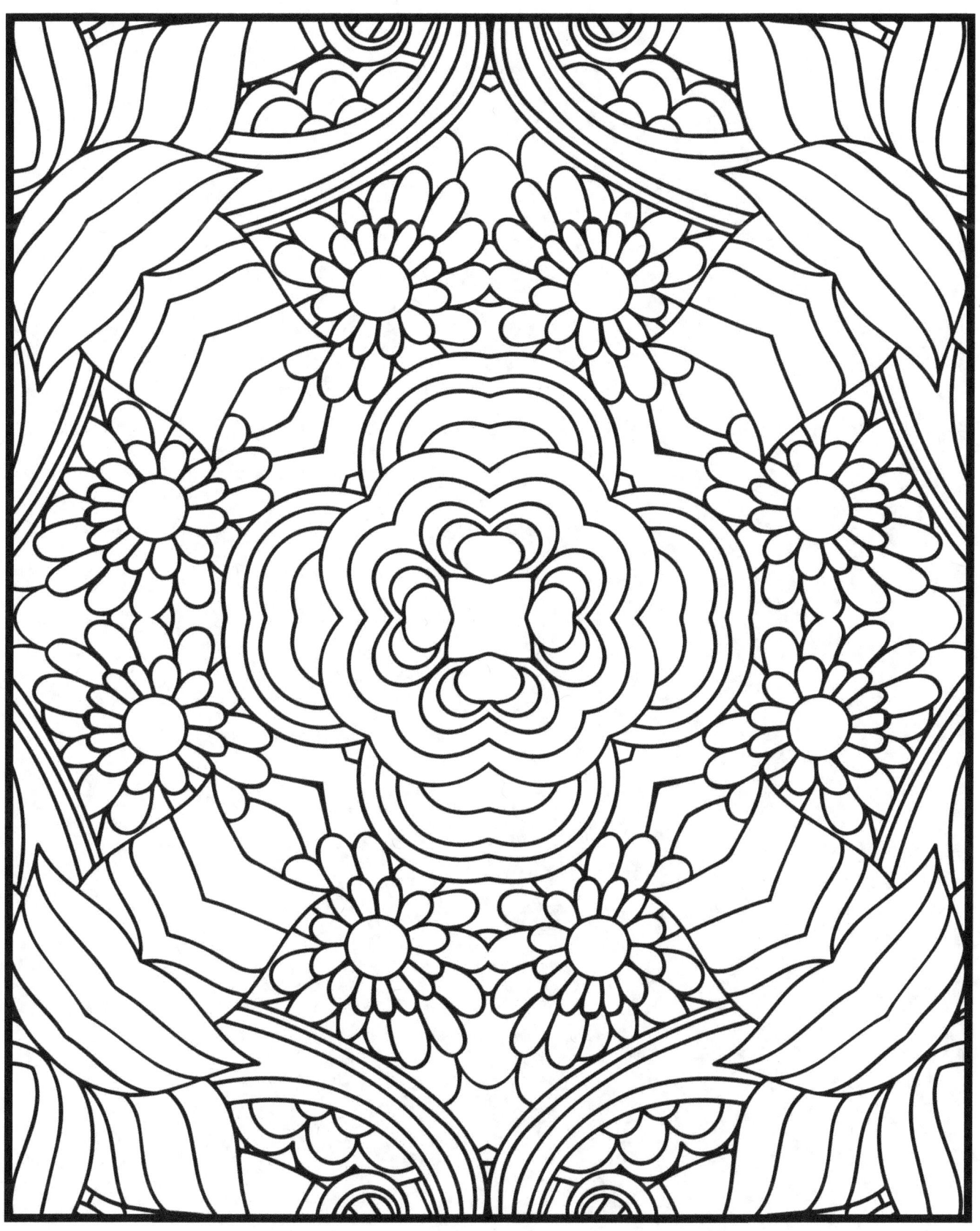

Design to Color.

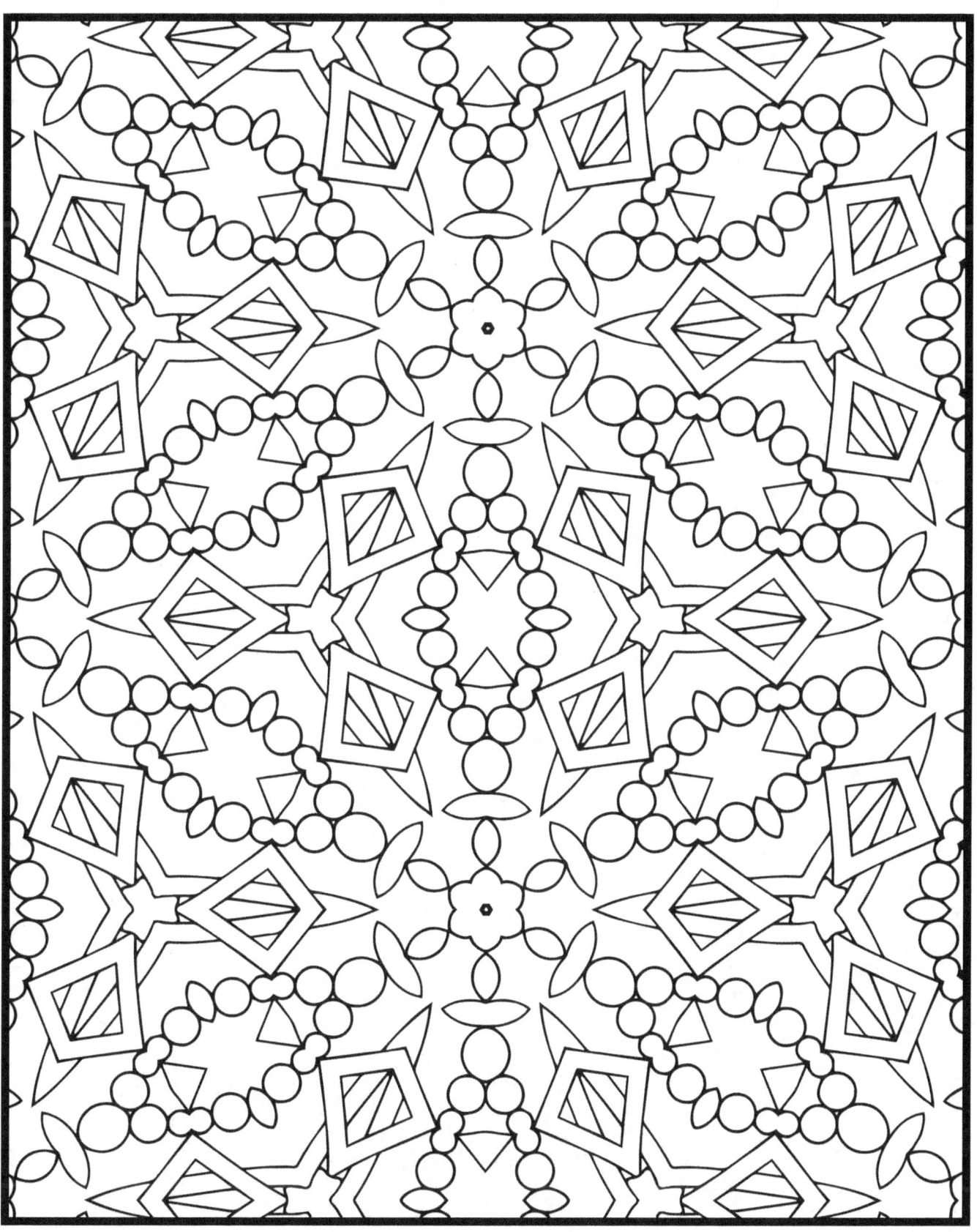

Design to Color.

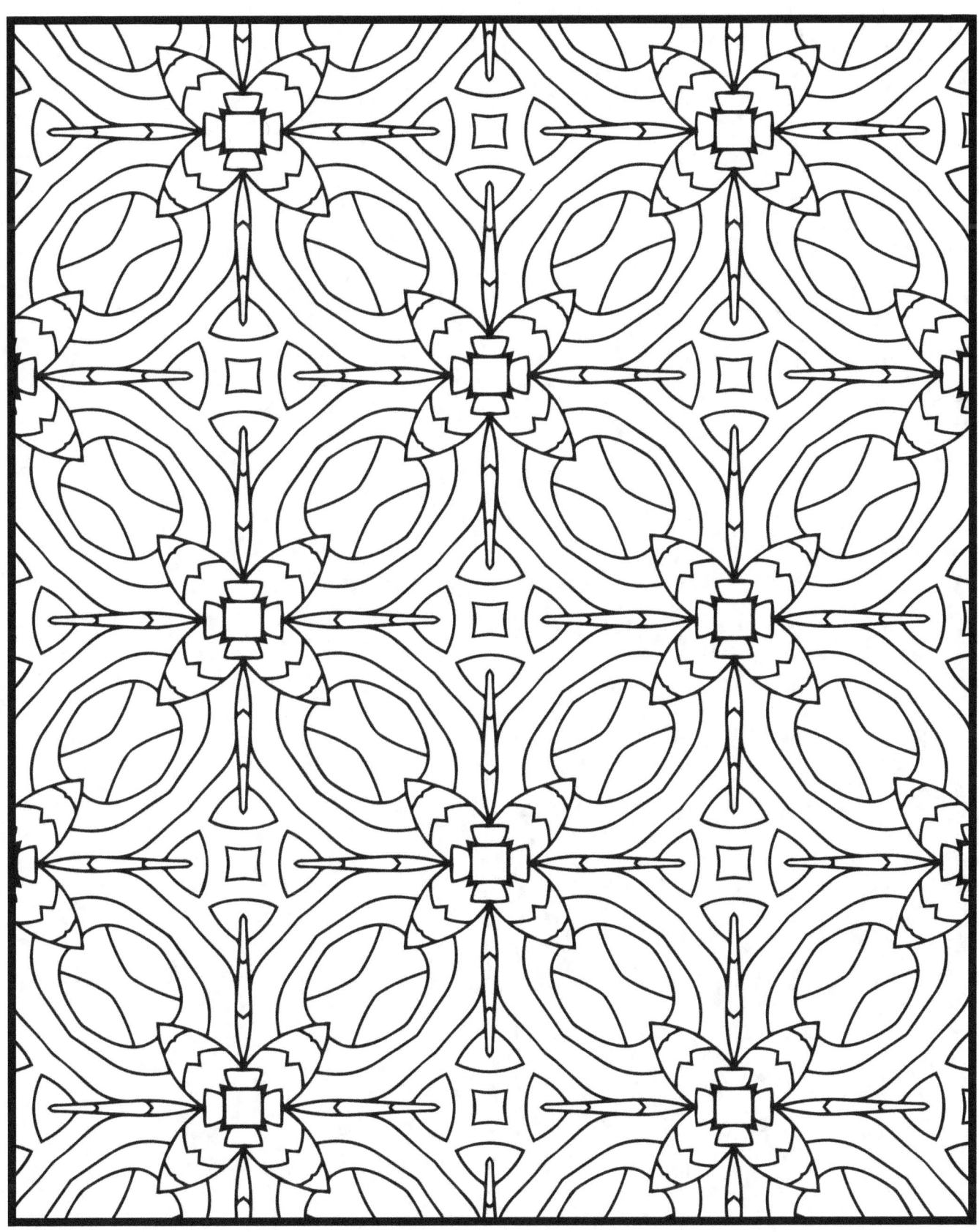

Design to Color.

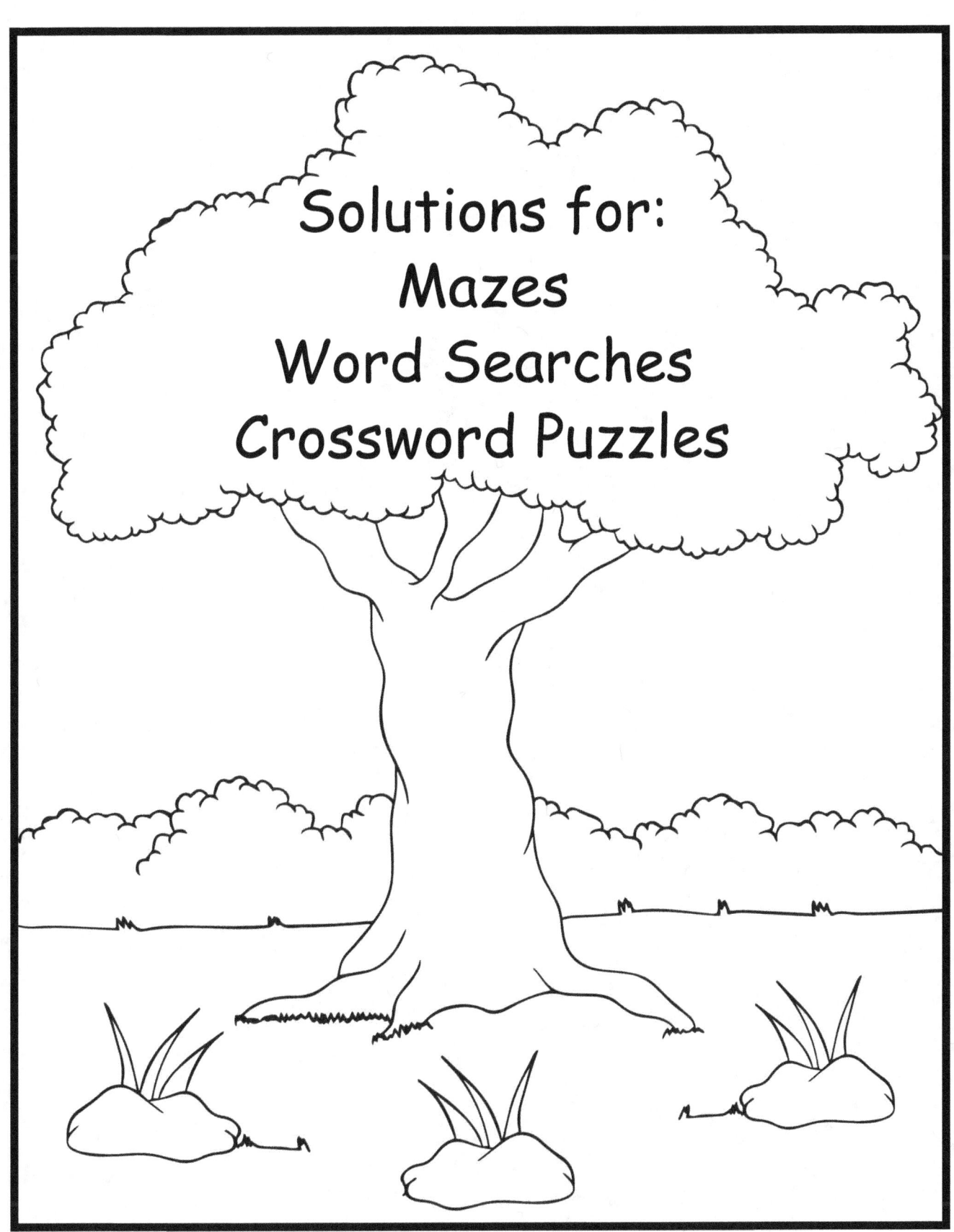

Solutions for:
Mazes
Word Searches
Crossword Puzzles

Solution for Izabel's Maze on page 27.

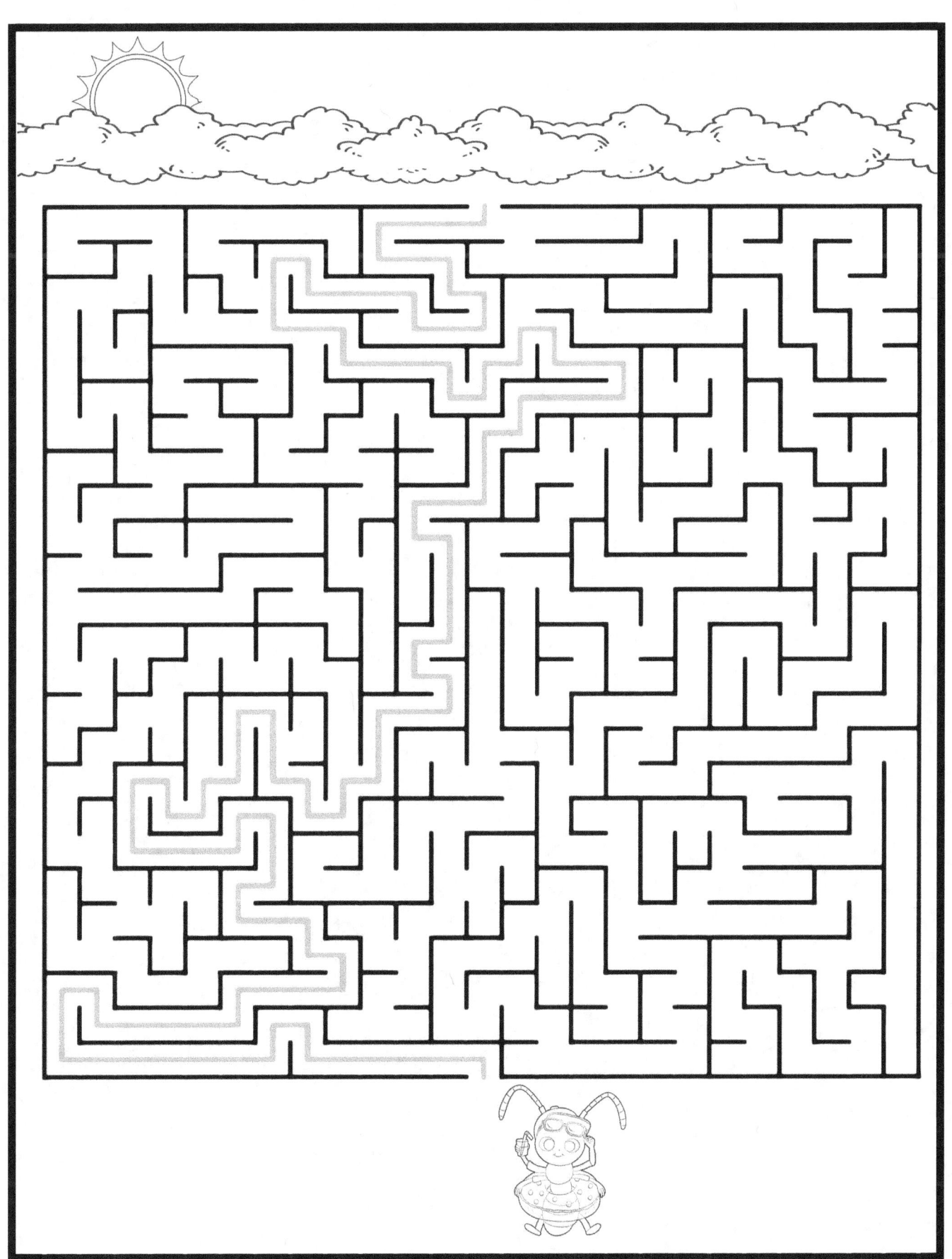

Solution for Victor's Maze on page 29.

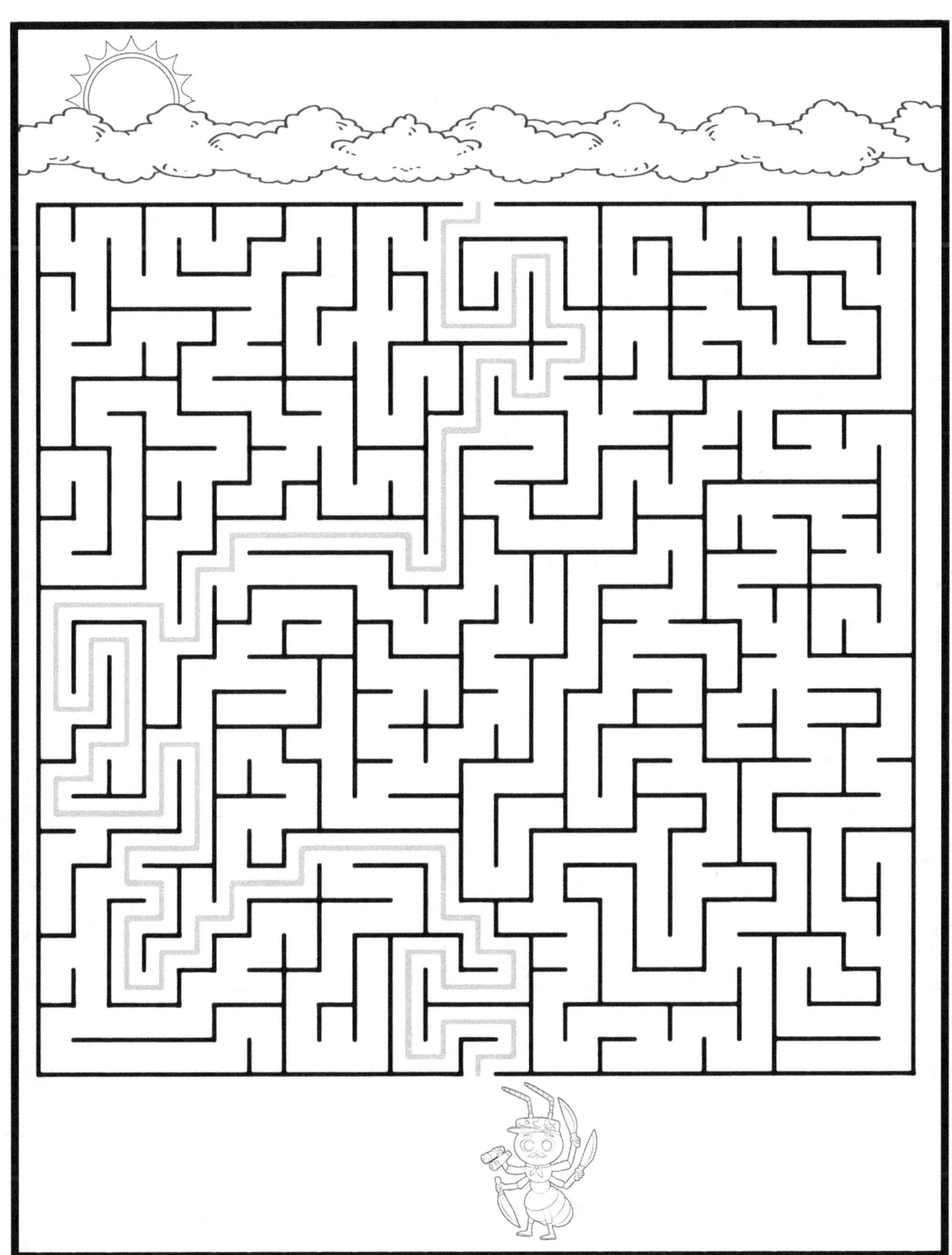

Solution for Mike's Maze on page 31.

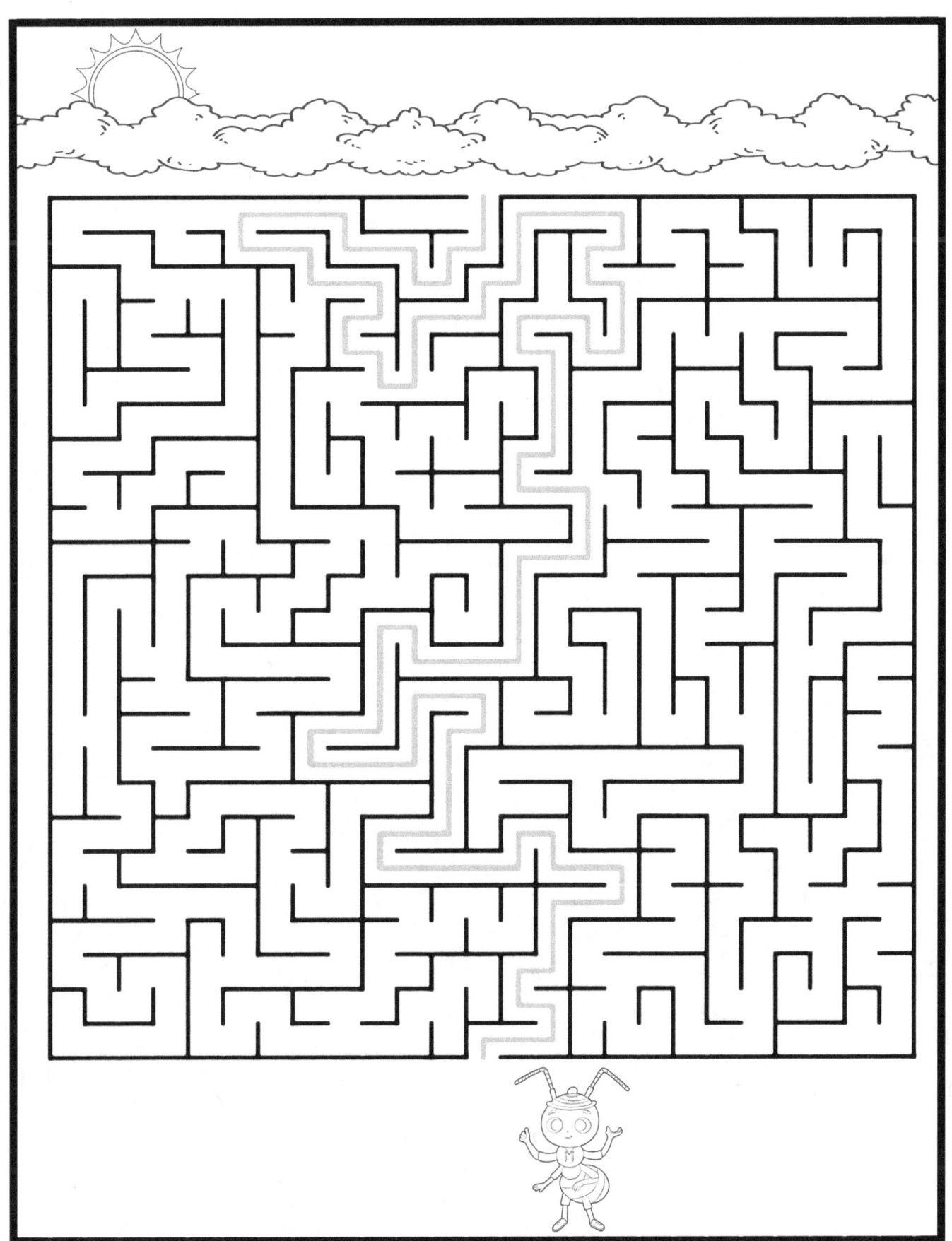

Solution for Wanda's Maze on page 33.

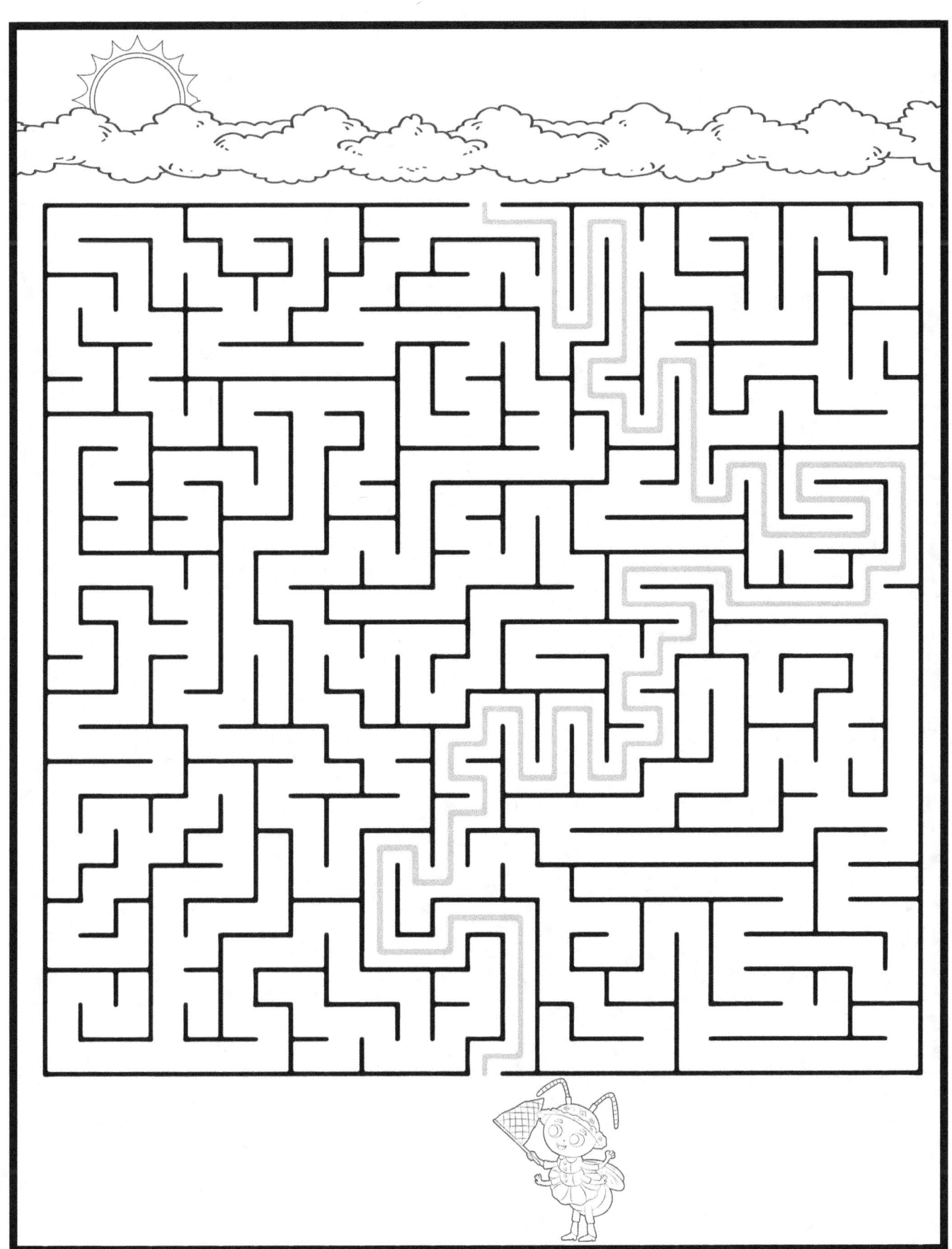

Solution for Edgar's Maze on page 35.

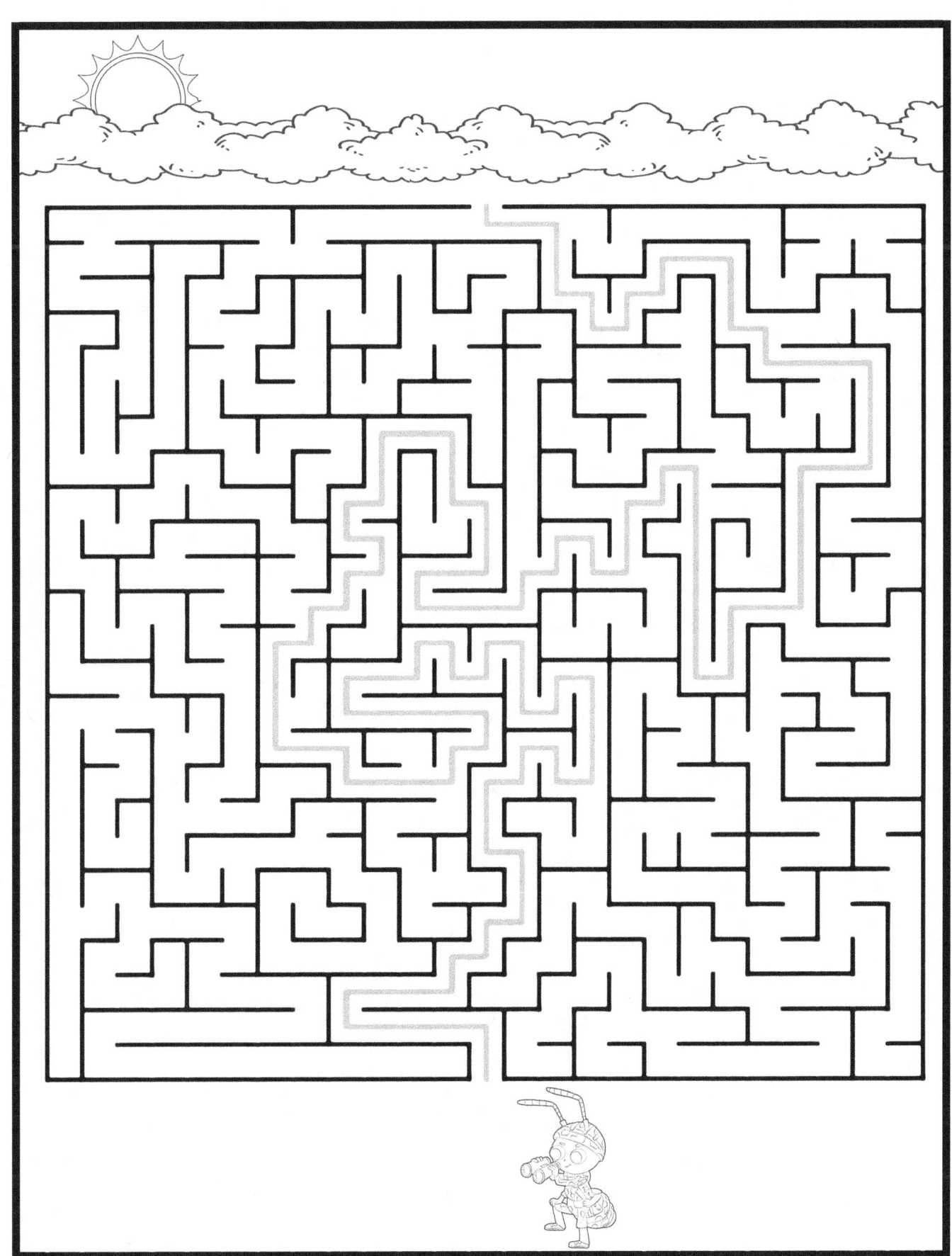

Solution for Liam's Maze on page 37.

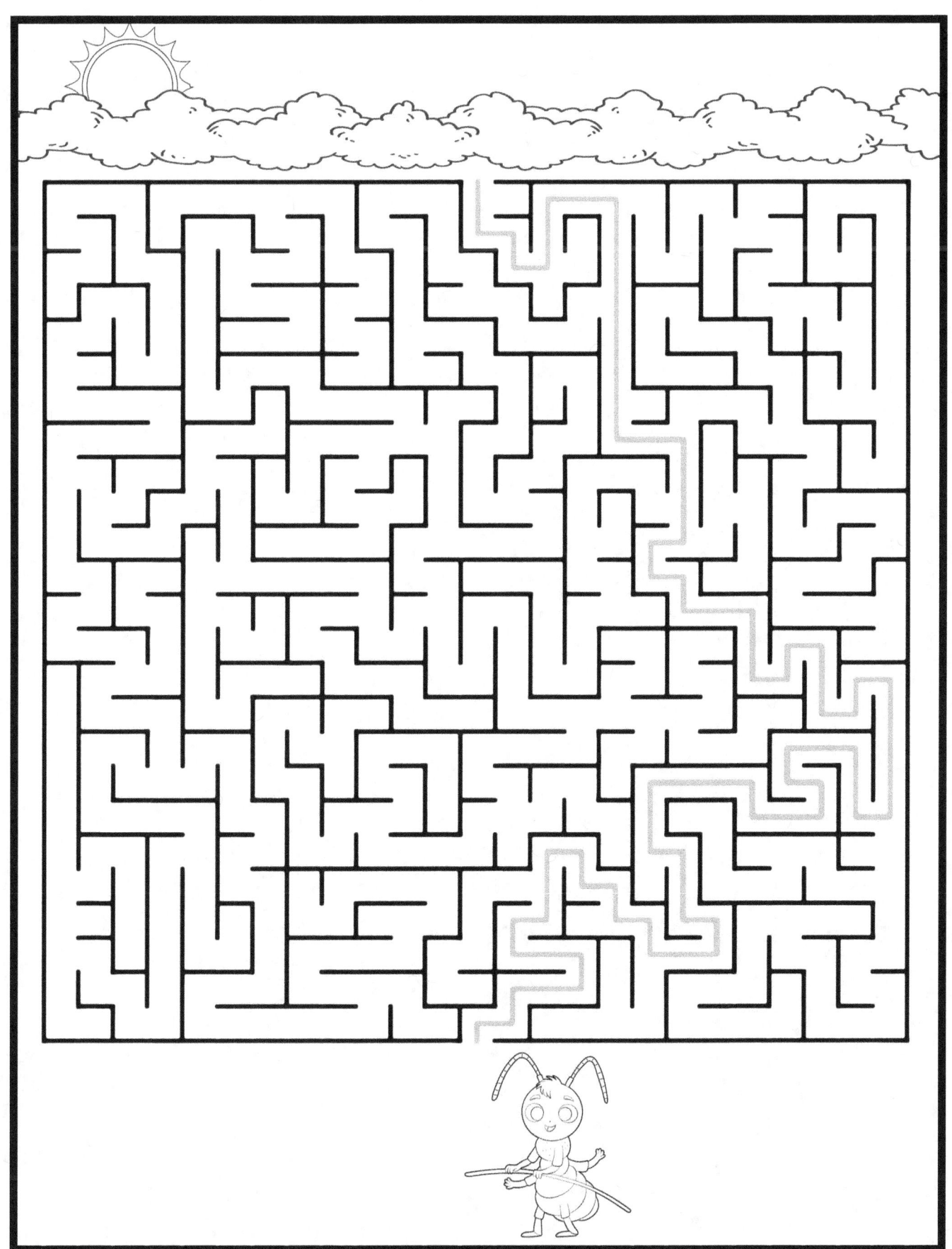

You can find a PDF of mazes in this book to download and more fun books relating to nature on Julia's ETSY shop at: https://www.etsy.com/shop/Fantafaces.

20 aMAZEing
Squirrely Fun Puzzles

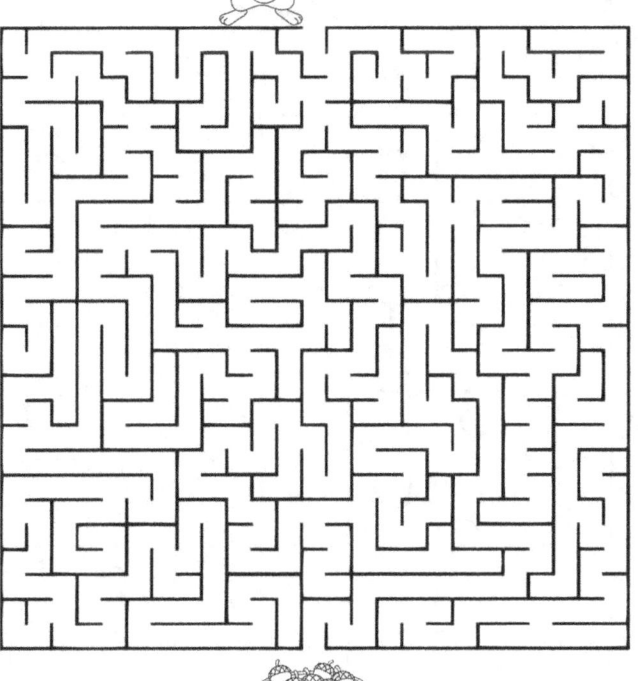

Cute Chipmunks, Fun-loving Squirrels, Lovely Butterflies and Adventurous Ants Need Your Help to Discover the Paths to Acorns, Flowers or an Exit from an Anthill.

5 Chipmunk Mazes

5 Butterfly Mazes

5 Squirrel Mazes

5 Ant Mazes

A printable book of MAZES related to the "Critter Activity Book" collection created by

Julia L Wright

HieroGraphics Books

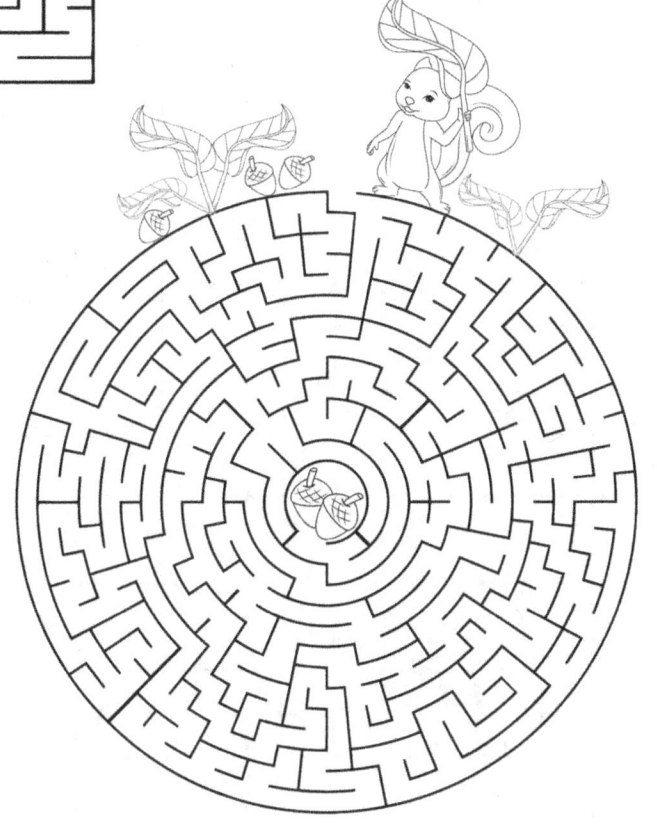

Solution for the Adventurous Ants Names Word Search Puzzle on Page 55.

- __ ANNIE
- __ BERRI
- __ CIARA
- __ EDGAR
- __ IZABEL
- __ LIAM
- __ MIKE
- __ OLIVIA
- __ PETER
- __ QUINTON
- __ VICTOR
- __ WANDA
- __ XAVIER
- __ YOLANDI
- __ ZARA

					X		A	P			R		
				A		R	E	I	N	N	A		
			V		A			T			G		
B		I			I	Z	A	B	E	L	D		
	E		C					R			E		
R		R	A							E	K	I	M
		A			I			Q	R				
	Z				V	U	I	D	N	A	L	O	Y
					I							L	
				N	L	C						I	
			T		I			T				V	
			O		A			O				I	
W	A	N	D	A	M					R		A	

Solution for the Adventurous Ants
Glossary Word Search Puzzle on Page 57.

__ APPLE
__ ASTRONAUT
__ BEEHIVE
__ BUTTERFLY
__ BIRTHDAY

__ CASTLE
__ CEREMONY
__ FRIENDS
__ FLOWERS
__ HARVEST

__ JUNGLE
__ MACHETE
__ PLANTING
__ SHOVEL
__ WATERMELON

							Y	L	F	R	E	T	T	U	B	
E	V	I	H	E	E	B									I	
	L		E	L	G	N	U	J				L			R	
		T		P		S						E			T	
T			S	P		R						V			H	
U			W	A	T	E	R	M	E	L	O	N			D	
A	H			C	W			A			H	S			A	
N		A			O				C	S	D			Y		
O			R		L				H	N						
R			V		F				E							
T			C	E	R	E	M	O	N	Y	I	T				
S				S					R		E					
A		G	N	I	T	N	A	L	P	F						

Answers for the Adventurous Ants Names Crossword Puzzle.

ACROSS

4. Who is bringing a cake to a birthday celebration? **CIARA**
5. Who is carrying machetes to explore the jungle? **VICTOR**
8. Who is using binoculars to watch bees and butterflies? **EDGAR**
9. Who is dancing around a fire in a mountain valley? **ZARA**
11. Who is practicing walking on a tightwire? **LIAM**
12. Who is reading a book on a hammock? **YOLANDI**
15. Who is bringing a cupcake to a birthday celebration? **OLIVIA**
16. Who is picking apples by a barn? **MIKE**

DOWN

1. Who traveled to the moon? **XAVIER**
2. Who planted a lot of flowers in his garden? **PETER**
3. Who is enjoying eating slices of a watermelon? **BERRIE**
6. Who went looking to capture butterflies in a net? **WANDA**
7. Who floated down a river in an inner tube? **IZABEL**
10. Who used a big leaf to fly around the forest? **QUINTON**
13. Who is on a path to visit a castle in the sky? **ANNIE**
14. Who is playing disco music? **GALE**

Solution for the Adventurous Ants Names Crossword Puzzle on page 73.

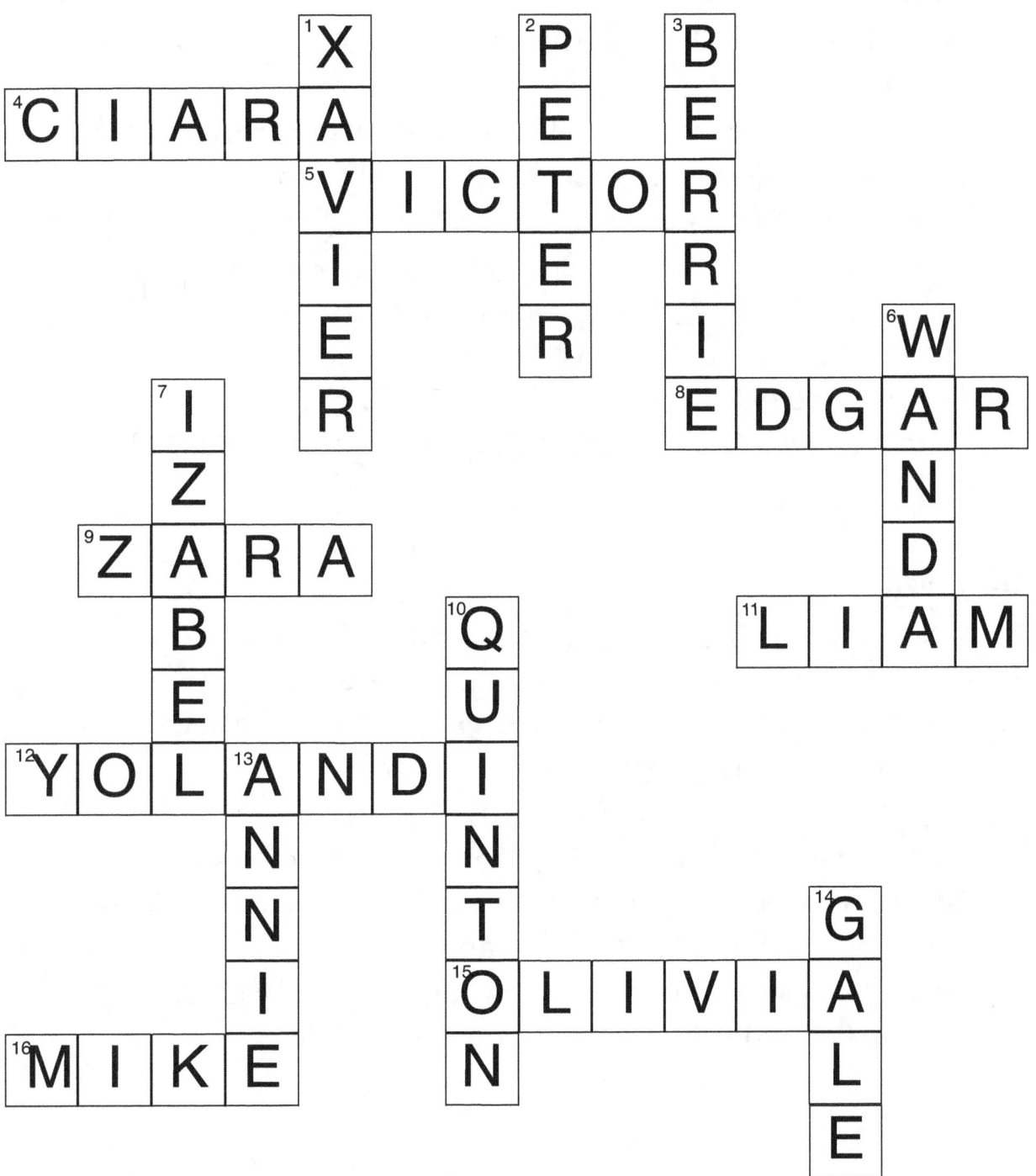

Answers for the Adventurous Ants Glossary Word Crossword Puzzle.

ACROSS

2. Xavier is an **ASTRONAUT** who went into outer space in a rocket.
4. Xavier traveled to the **MOON** on his big adventure.
5. Olivia brought a cupcake to a field of flowers for her **BIRTHDAY**.
7. Liam used a **POLE** to balance himself on a tightrope.
8. Annie dressed as a fairy princess went to a **CASTLE** in the night sky.
10. Izabel traveled in an inner tube to **FLOAT** down a river.
11. Peter was busy **PLANTING** flowers on a sunny day.
13. Edgar took a map of the **FOREST** to find a bee hive.
16. Berri enjoyed eating slices of a **WATERMELON**.
19. Ciara brought a Cake to **CELEBRATE** her birthday with Olivia.

DOWN

1. Victor carried a **MACHETE** on his adventure in a jungle.
2. Mike went to pick **APPLES** on a tree near a barn.
3. A rainbow is arched over the **MOUNTAINS** behind Quinton.
6. Yolandi enjoyed **READING** a book in a hammock.
9. Wanda left the anthill carrying a **BUTTERFLY** net.
12. Peter spent a day planting **FLOWERS** in his garden.
14. Zara was dancing around a fire near a **RIVER** in a mountain valley.
15. Mike stood on hay **BALES** to pick apples.
17. Edgar used his binoculars to watch butterflies and **BEES**.
18. Quinton flew around the forest using a big **LEAF**.

Solution for the Adventurous Ants
Glossary Word Crossword Puzzle on page 75.

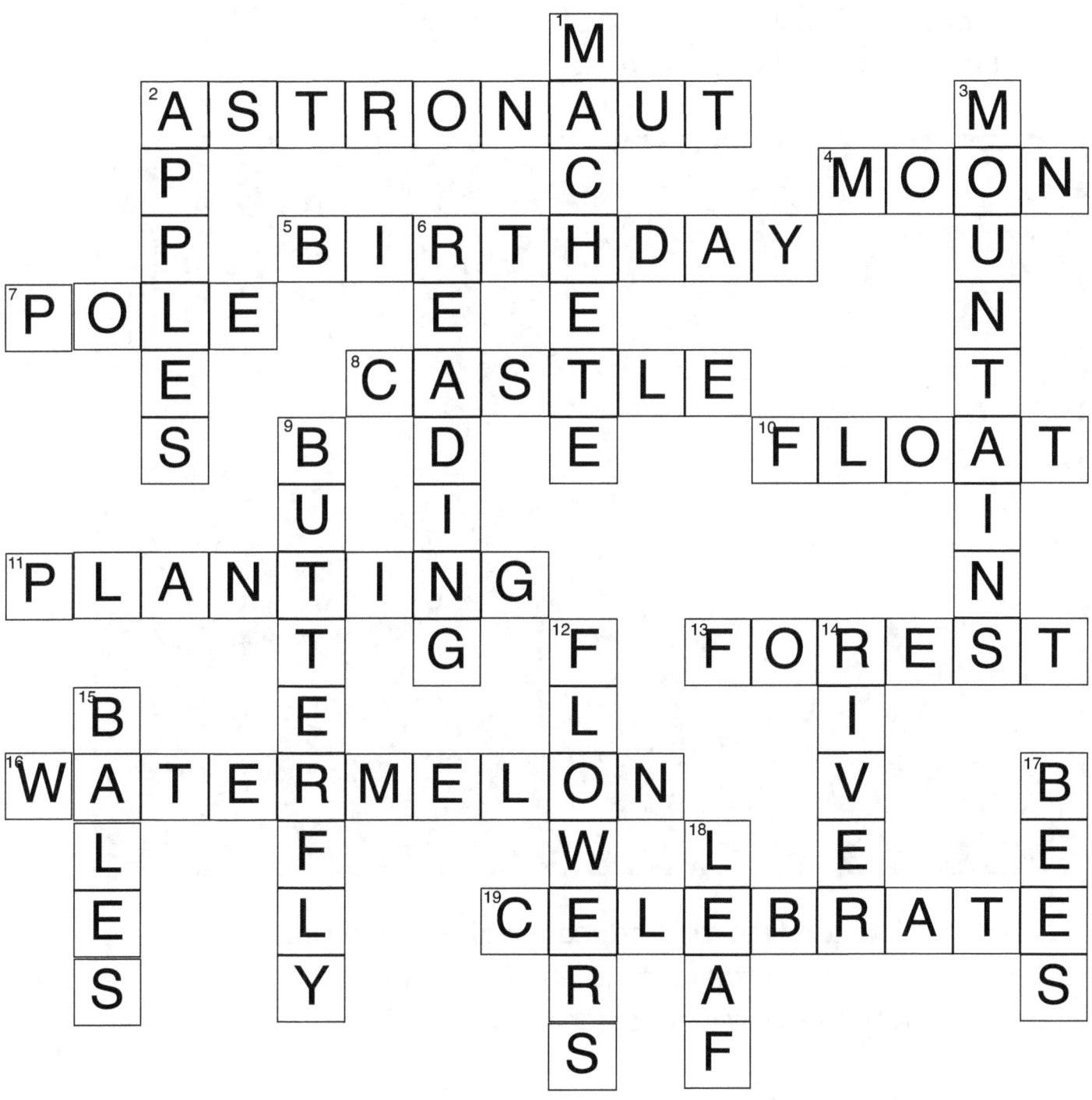

If you love bugs and butterflies, chances are you also enjoy watching squirrels at play. In Violet Burbach's and Julia L. Wright's colorfully illustrated book, "Discover The World Of Squirrels", children can learn interesting facts about these fascinating creatures that live in forests around the world.

This book includes a glossary of new words kids will be introduced to when reading the book.

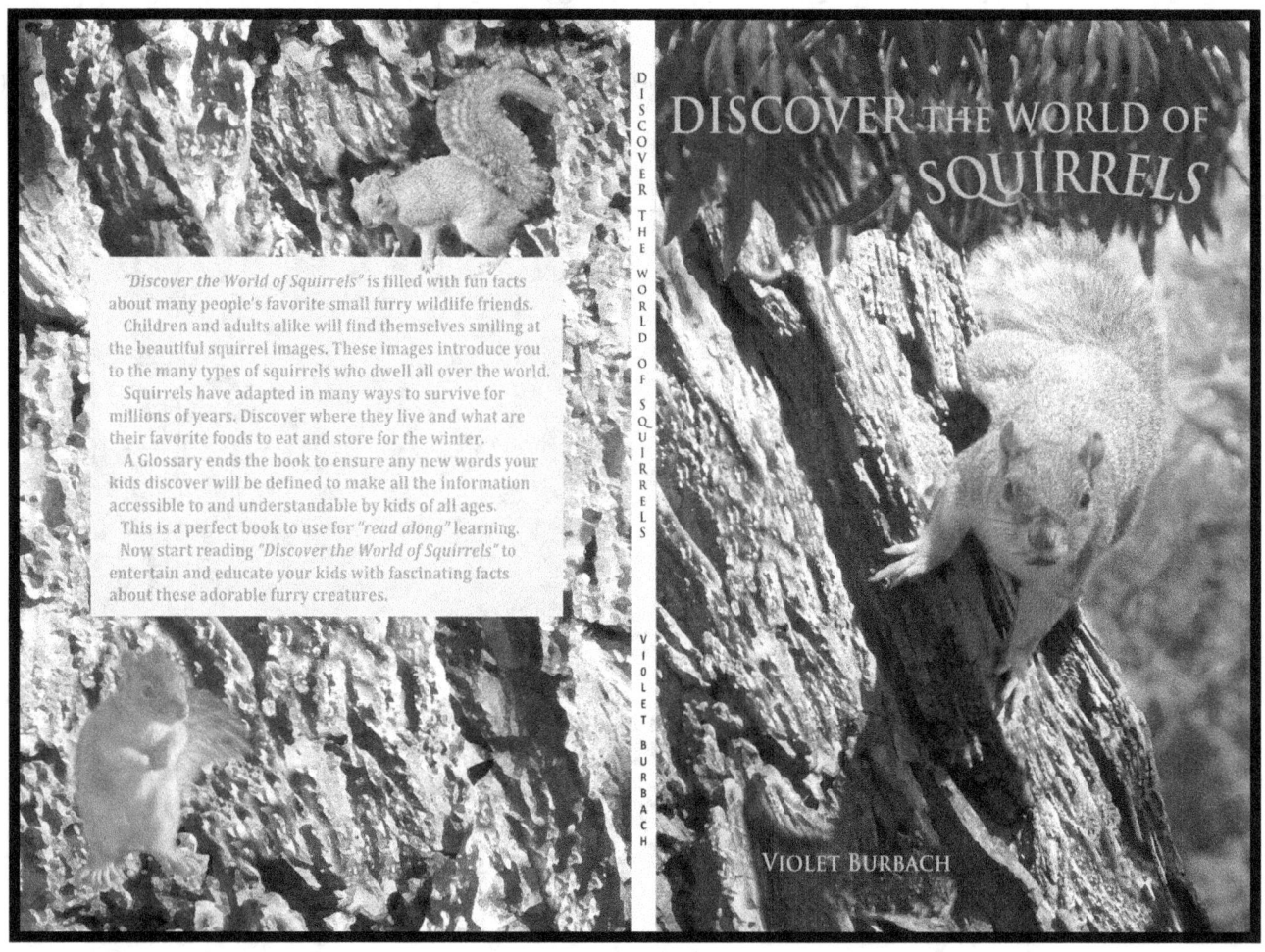

You can find this educational and fun book
about squirrels on Amazon at:
https://www.amazon.com/dp/1512255335/

And if you want to learn more about chipmunks and other ground squirrels check out "Discover The World Of Ground Squirrels" at: https://www.amazon.com/dp/0996581634.

Rockey is inviting you to come explore the "Squirrel Coloring And Activity Book" from HieroGraphics Books.
www.amazon.com/dp/0996581669/

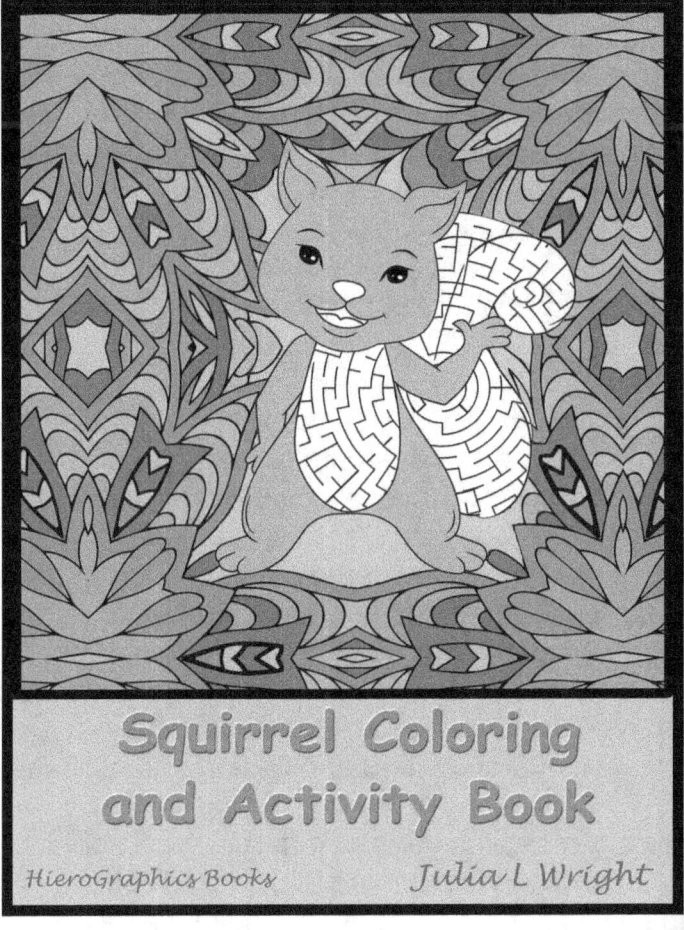

Princess Acorna would like to invite you to come explore the "Chipmunk Coloring And Activity Book" from HieroGraphics Books.
www.amazon.com/dp/0996581650/

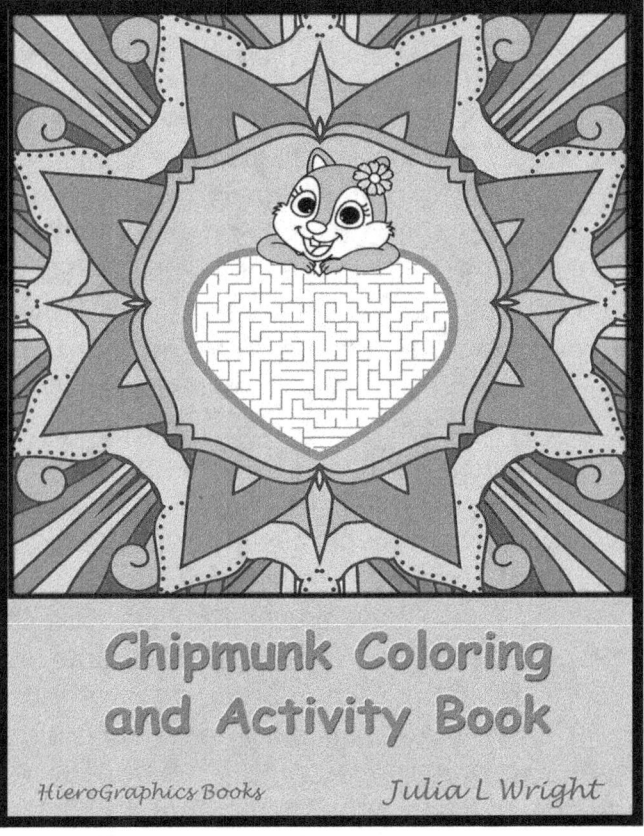

You will find these, and other coloring and activity books created by Julia L. Wright on Amazon.com.

Click on my author name to find more coloring and activities books filled with cute critters and mandalas for hours of fun.

Fun and Interesting Facts about Ants

Ants are among Earth's most successful creatures, having thrived for over 150 million years. These tiny architects have built some of the most complex societies in the animal kingdom, demonstrating that size doesn't determine significance in nature's grand design.

Almost every language around the world has at least one word describing ants. All of these words come from West Germanic æmaitjōn, and the original meaning of the word was "the biter".

Ants vary in color; most ants are yellow to red or brown to black, but a few species are green and some tropical species have a metallic luster. Ants range in size from 0.030–2.0 inches. Ant colonies can be long-lived. The queens can live for up to 30 years, and workers live from 1 to 3 years. Males, however, are more transitory, being quite short-lived and surviving for only a few weeks. Ant queens are estimated to live 100 times as long as solitary insects of a similar size.

Ants have colonies on almost every landmass on Earth except Antarctica and a few remote or inhospitable islands. Ants thrive in moist tropical ecosystems and may exceed the combined biomass of wild birds and mammals. More than 13,800 species are currently known, with the greatest diversity in the tropics. Ants are active all year long in the tropics; however, in cooler regions, they survive the winter in hibernation. The forms of inactivity are varied and species have larvae going into the inactive state, while in others, the adults alone pass the winter in a state of reduced activity.

Ants evolved from wasp-like ancestors during the mid-Cretaceous period, roughly the same time dinosaurs roamed the Earth. The oldest known ant fossil, Sphecomyrma freyi, was discovered preserved in amber and shows the transitional features between ants and their wasp predecessors. This evolutionary leap occurred when some wasps abandoned their solitary lifestyle and embraced the power of cooperation. For millions of years, they were a relatively minor player in the insect world. However, around 100 million years ago, a major ecological shift occurred with the rise of flowering plants. As these plants created complex, dense forest canopies, they provided a buffet of new resources on the forest floor, from fallen leaves to nectar and new prey. Ants capitalized on this new ecosystem, branching out into thousands of different species.

When the asteroid struck Earth 66 million years ago, wiping out the non-avian dinosaurs, the resilient ants went deep underground. They survived the ensuing nuclear winter and emerged into a world they would thrive in. Today, there are over 15,000 described species of ants, and likely thousands more waiting to be discovered.

What sets ants apart is their eusocial structure. Ants exhibit one of nature's most sophisticated forms of organization. Ants are eusocial insects, meaning they live in highly organized, cooperative societies. An Ant colony is what scientists often refer to an ant colony as a "superorganism", where individual ants sacrifice personal reproduction for the colony's success.

All ant colonies consist of various castes of sterile, wingless females, most of which are workers, as well as soldiers and other specialized groups. The Queen is the beating heart of the colony. Queens are larger than other ants and possess wings until they mate. After a "nuptial flight" where she mates with males, a queen sheds her wings, burrows into the ground, and begins a new colony. Her sole job is to lay eggs. Ant queens are the longest-living insects on Earth. Some have been known to live for up to 30 years. The Worker ants are sterile females that make up the vast majority of the colony. They gather the food, defend the nest, expand tunnels, and nurse the young. Depending on the species, workers may be further divided into "minors" (nurses) and "majors" (soldiers). The Males, also known as Drones, are short-lived individuals that have only one purpose ant that is to mate with a new queen. They are born with wings, take part in the nuptial flight, and die shortly after mating.

The size of colonies ants create range in size. The smallest ones have a few dozen individuals living in small natural cavities. Larger and highly organized colonies that may occupy large territories with a sizeable nest or nests that consist of millions of individuals. In some cases there may be hundreds of millions of individual ants living in super colonies. These colonies are considered to be superorganisms because the ants appear to operate as a unified entity. abd they collectively work together to support the colony.

Ants communicate primarily through a complex vocabulary of chemicals called pheromones. When a worker ant finds a food source, she leaves a temporary chemical trail on her way back to the nest. Other ants follow this trail, reinforcing the scent with their own pheromones as long as the food lasts. Pheromones are also used to sound the alarm when the colony is attacked, to identify intruders, and to determine which dead ants need to be carried to the colony's "graveyard." Through their antennae, an ant's sense of smell is incredibly sharp, allowing them to decode these messages instantly. Ants identify kin and nest mates through their scent, which comes from hydrocarbon-laced secretions that coat their exoskeletons. If an ant is separated from its original colony, it will eventually lose the colony scent. Any ant that enters a colony without a matching scent will be attacked.

Relationship with humans

Ants perform many ecological roles that are beneficial to humans. Ants serve as nature's cleanup crew, soil aerators, and seed dispersers. They consume vast quantities of dead organic matter, control pest populations, and some species are so integral to their ecosystems that their disappearance would trigger ecological collapse. Ants also turn and aerate more soil than earthworms, redistributing nutrients and allowing water to reach plant roots. It has been estimated that an average of about 1.5 tons of subsoil are moved to the surface by ants per year per hectare.

Many plants have evolved to produce seeds with lipid-rich appendages specifically to attract ants. The ants carry the seeds underground, eat the appendage, and leave the seed planted in nutrient-rich soil. As fierce predators, ants control the populations of other insects, preventing unchecked outbreaks of pests that would otherwise decimate vegetation. In South Africa, ants are used to help harvest the seeds of rooibos, a plant used to make a herbal tea. The plant disperses its seeds widely, making manual collection difficult. Black ants collect and store these and other seeds in their nest, where humans can gather them en masse. Up to half a pound of seeds may be collected from one ant-heap.

Ants have been the model of choice for the study of questions on the evolution of social systems because of their complex and varied forms of social organization. Their diversity and prominence in ecosystems also has made them important components in the study of biodiversity and conservation. The successful techniques used by ant colonies have been studied in computer science and robotics to produce distributed and fault-tolerant systems for solving problems, for example Ant colony optimization and Ant robotics. This area of biomimetics has led to studies of ant locomotion, search engines that make use of "foraging trails", fault-tolerant storage, and networking algorithms.

Many human cultures make use of ants in cuisine, medication, and rites. Some species are valued in their role as biological pest control agents. Although their ability to exploit resources has brought some ants into conflict with humans, as they can damage crops and invade buildings.

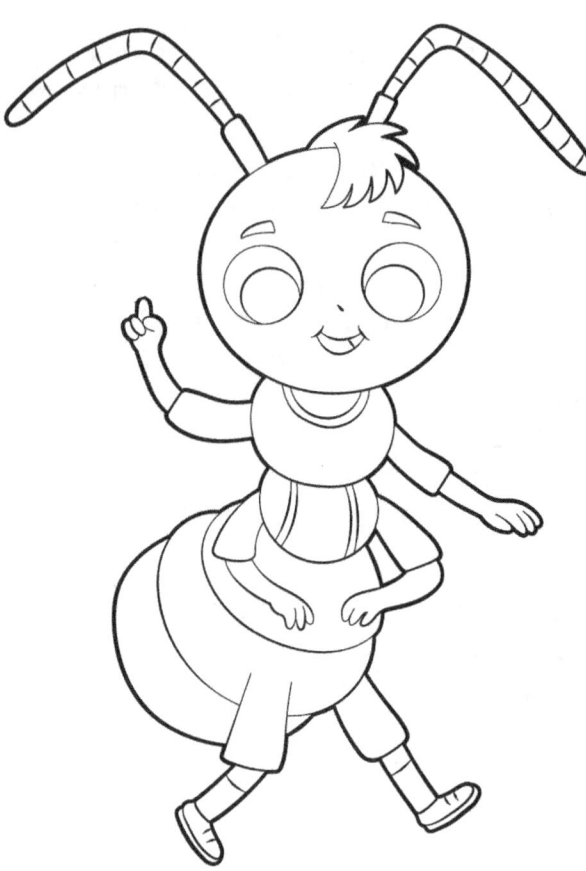

Ants in Culture

Anthropomorphised ants have often been used in fables, children's stories, and religious texts to represent industriousness and cooperative effort, such as in the Aesop fable The Ant and the Grasshopper. In parts of Africa, ants are considered to be the messengers of the deities. Some Native American mythology, such as the Hopi mythology, considers ants as the first animals. In Greek mythology, the goddess Athena turned the maiden Myrmex into an ant when the latter claimed to have invented the plough, when in fact it was Athena's own invention.

Ant bites are used in the initiation ceremonies of some Amazon Indian cultures as a test of endurance. Whereas in other places, ant bites are often said to have curative properties. The sting of some species of Pseudomyrmex is claimed to give fever relief.

Ants also are quite popular inspiration for many science-fiction insectoids, such as the "Bugs of Starship Troopers", the giant ants in the films "Them!" and as Marvel Comics' super hero Ant-Man. In computer strategy games, ant-based species often benefit from increased production rates due to their single-minded focus. These characters are often credited with a hive mind, a common misconception about ant colonies.

From the late 1950s through the late 1970s, ant farms were popular educational children's toys in the United States. Some later commercial versions use transparent gel instead of soil, allowing greater visibility at the cost of stressing the ants with unnatural light.

In Conclusion

Ants are a testament to the power of cooperation. The next time you see ants marching in formation, remember that you are you witnessing one of evolution's greatest achievements in action. Ant societies have division of Labor, communication between individuals, and an ability to solve complex problems. As we face environmental challenges, ants offer valuable lessons in sustainability, cooperation, and efficient resource management. Their 150-million-year success story reminds us that sometimes the smallest creatures cast the longest shadows in the story of life on Earth.

Now is the Time For You to Color or Write a Story or Draw a Ant

Think about how no snowflakes are alike, and set in motion your creativity by coloring each one in this book however you choose. Each time you color one of the ants in this book, you create a unique version of this fanciful creature that will never be the same as another one. What story might you write about a ant? Or draw and color to illustrate an idea in that story? Have Fun!

Give your story a title using the Adventurous Ant's name and what he or she is doing. Then have fun telling a story about what this bug will do next, starting with the scene on the page you are writing this story about.

TITLE: _____

_____

_____

_____

_____

_____

_____

_____

_____

_____

_____

_____

_____

Aspiring artists can use this page to create an image for your story.

Give your story a title using the Adventurous Ant's name and what he or she is doing. Then have fun telling a story about what this bug will do next, starting with the scene on the page you are writing this story about.

TITLE: _____

_____

_____

_____

_____

_____

_____

_____

_____

_____

_____

_____

_____

Aspiring artists can use this page to create an image for your story.

Give your story a title using the Adventurous Ant's name and what he or she is doing. Then have fun telling a story about what this bug will do next, starting with the scene on the page you are writing this story about.

TITLE: _____

_____

_____

_____

_____

_____

_____

_____

_____

_____

_____

_____

_____

_____

Aspiring artists can use this page to create an image for your story.

Give your story a title using the Adventurous Ant's name and what he or she is doing. Then have fun telling a story about what this bug will do next, starting with the scene on the page you are writing this story about.

TITLE: _____

_____

_____

_____

_____

_____

_____

_____

_____

_____

_____

_____

_____

_____

Aspiring artists can use this page to create an image for your story.

Give your story a title using the Adventurous Ant's name and what he or she is doing. Then have fun telling a story about what this bug will do next, starting with the scene on the page you are writing this story about.

TITLE: _____

_____

_____

_____

_____

_____

_____

_____

_____

_____

_____

_____

_____

_____

www.ingramcontent.com/pod-product-compliance
Lightning Source LLC
Chambersburg PA
CBHW080415290526
45791CB00008BA/2283